ART TREASURES
OF ITALY

ART TREASURES OF ITALY

Bernard Denvir

Galahad Books • New York City

Opposite GIOVANNI BATTISTA CIMA
DA CONEGLIANO called CIMA
(1459/60–1517/18)
The Madonna of the Orange Tree
Panel, $83\frac{1}{4} \times 54\frac{1}{2}$ in (212 × 139 cm)
Gallerie dell' Accademia, Venice

The Venetian feeling for the mysterious beauty of landscape is movingly shown in this 'sacred conversation piece'. Cima characteristically prefers to contrast landscape and figures in a curiously arbitrary way.

VITTORE CARPACCIO
(c. 1460/5–1523/6)
The Martrydom of St. Ursula
Oil on canvas, $107\frac{3}{4} \times 208\frac{3}{4}$ in (274 × 561 cm)
Gallerie dell' Accademia, Venice

In this complex scene, with its many figures and differing episodes drawn together into one composition, can be seen the influence of Signorelli's manipulation of crowd scenes.

Violence was not perhaps the easiest of subjects for Carpaccio to deal with but there is, however, something powerful about the impassive kneeling figures.

© Orbis Publishing Limited, London 1980
Published by A&W Publishers Inc.,
95 Madison Avenue, New York 10016
ISBN: 0 88365 451 2
Library of Congress Catalog Card Number: 80 81300

Printed in Czechoslovakia

CONTENTS

Introduction

ART IS NOT something which just happens. It is a flowering nurtured from a rich compost of historical, social and personal interaction. It is created by genius and inspiration, but those gifts, though they reflect the personalities of individuals, can only find expression through patronage, through demand and through systems of artistic education. For most of history, art as we know it today did not exist. It was not to be appreciated as something distinct from the functioning of everyday life, from the transmission of religious beliefs or the attempt to master a hostile and intransigent environment. It is only during the past few centuries that its manifestations have come to be regarded as the sacred objects of a secular culture, carefully preserved in museums, cosseted with reverential awe and discussed endlessly. Today art is viewed by countless millions who visit museums and galleries with the same kind of awed dedication as that which inspired the shrine-haunting pilgrims of the Middle Ages.

This book is intended to reflect something of this complex interplay of factors in relation to one specific aspect of the European cultural heritage, the art treasures of Italy. It is not a history of Italian art, though inevitably it deals with that remarkable phenomenon, nor is it a catalogue of the contents of certain museums and art galleries. What I have attempted to do is to relate how in one country, over a period of nearly three thousand years, a language of visual expression grew up, nurtured by a social and historical environment which endowed it with specific characteristics. Despite the fact these characteristics varied from age to age and from century to century they always displayed a kind of family resemblance. These manifestations of Italian art have come into being for a wide variety of reasons: personal glorification, religious fervour, political propaganda, greed and sheer delight in beauty. Its creators have been men as diverse in their characters as mankind itself: avaricious, neurotic, idealistic, indolent, hard-working, ambitious and retiring, but all spurred by the accidents of their lives and the pressure of their circumstances into producing those objects which have become for us talismans of immortality.

Creatively the great artist is both the child of the past and the father of the future and in this particular context Italy has always offered unique advantages. In no other European country has the indigenous art of the past been so clearly in evidence throughout its history. The lure of Rome alone has captivated mens' minds for centuries and the words which Petrarch used in March 1337 after his first visit to that city, have been echoed by millions since:

> 'As I recall it, you were against my visiting Rome, warning me that the sight of the ruined city would contrast too sadly with all that I had read and heard about her, so that my fervent enthusiasm would dwindle. And I myself was not disinclined to postpone my visit in spite of my great longing, because I feared that the sight before my eyes would belittle the image

formed in my mind. Reality is always the enemy of famous names. But this time, oh wonder, reality has diminished nothing, but exceeded everything. Truly, Rome was grander than I had thought, grander too are her ruins! I am no longer astonished that this city has conquered the world. I am only surprised at its happening so late.'[1]

And Rome was only the *prima inter pares*, one of the many cities – Florence, Venice, Siena, Padua, Naples, Ravenna, Orvieto, Viterbo, Mantua, Urbino – the names of which have become part of the history of art. In such cities the icons of history are everywhere, part of the scenery of life and the fact that for centuries Italian painters and sculptors have been brought up in this great treasure house of the living past is one of the most important things that has moulded their creativity and enriched their vision. That too is why it has attracted so many artists from other countries – men such as Dürer, Rubens and Van Dyck – whose works have been profoundly affected by their experience there.

No less important were the unequalled opportunities for patronage which Italy established. The shrewd dabblings in the art market of merchants such as the Datini, the imaginative flair of emigrant bankers such as the Portinari and the magnificent extravagance of the Medici are well known. Of equal significance was the unexpected passion for collecting which informed a hard-bitten soldier of fortune such as Federigo da Montefeltro, the insatiable lust for possessing works of art which drove Isabella d'Este and the informed connoisseurship of Cardinal Scipione Borghese. These are but the highlights of a remarkable tradition which did not die with the eighteenth century. The art treasures of Italy, as we know them today, survive as they do thanks to the efforts of countless dedicated enthusiasts. These were men such as the sculptor Canova who rescued the loot which Napoleon had shipped off to Paris. Another friend of the Italian heritage was Peter Edwards, an English resident in Venice who lovingly catalogued these works of art which had been appropriated by its greedier citizens for their private profit and who was largely responsible for creating the Accademia to house them. Similarly, we may turn with gratitude to John Ruskin who publicized the more neglected aspects of Italian art in passionate prose. In the late twentieth century museum curators, technologists and scientists have become the custodians of this fabulous trust, dedicating to its preservation a skill and devotion commensurate with the value of the legacy. As a result of the efforts of these and countless others, the art treasures of Italy are now the art treasures of the world.

I

The Classical Heritage

ITALY, A COUNTRY 116,286 square miles (291,087 sq km) in size, with a population of over fifty-one million, contains no less than 1392 public art galleries and museums, sixty per cent of which are mainly concerned with the fine arts. They range in size from small diocesan museums such as that at Pienza, which contains about twenty paintings – mostly of the early Sienese School, four illuminated manuscripts, a fourteenth-century English cope, and a miscellaneous collection of Etruscan and Roman antiquities, to galleries such as the Pitti and Uffizi in Florence, the Accademia in Venice, the Vatican Museums and Borghese Palace in Rome, whose collections of works of art are unparalleled in the whole world. Italy is the only country where you can find guide-book references containing such throw-away lines as 'in the adjacent rooms are paintings by Veronese, Tintoretto, Guardi and Tiepolo'. This is only a minute part of the country's cultural treasures. There are more than 100,000 monuments – cathedrals, churches, public statues, houses and archaeological sites – of outstanding historical significance. There is hardly a village church which does not contain a fresco, a painting, or a statue of some significance, hardly a monastery which does not count among its treasures fine, illuminated manuscripts, magnificent, golden altar vessels, beautifully embroidered vestments or altarpieces by a famous artist. No country in the world holds so many treasures – a source of pride to most of its inhabitants, of irritation to those few, who, like the Futurists of the 1920s, feel that the present is weighed down by the legacy of the living past.

Italy's past has indeed been remarkable. At least twice it has dominated the Western world and profoundly altered its structure and its way of life. In the opening centuries of our era the Roman Empire extended its language, its customs, its administrative systems, its ways of thought and its art over most of Europe, and in effect converted what had been little more than a peninsula of Asia into that continental unity which we know today. All Western nations, and many Eastern too, still bear the imprint of Rome in various ways, and the survival of the papacy itself, despite its claims to universality, as a very Italian institution perpetuates in the late twentieth century something of the imperial presence.

About fourteen centuries after the establishment of the Roman Empire, Italy once again put an emphatic imprint on the western world. That splendid creative explosion known as the Renaissance, laid the foundations of a culture which in its essentials, in the attitudes which it fostered, the cultural devices it exploited, the artistic idioms it evolved, has dominated the world ever since. In its inception and in its most magnificent manifestations, the Renaissance was predominantly an Italian pheno-menon. It is true that, in art for instance, it received some impetus from the northern countries, from painters such as the Van Eycks, Memling and Dürer, but this was slight in comparison with the local achievement of a whole host of artists from Giotto and

I

1. *Portrait of a Man and his Wife*
Fresco, $22\frac{3}{4} \times 20\frac{1}{2}$ in (58×52 cm)
Museo Nazionale, Naples

Similar in feeling to the wax mummy portraits of Roman Egypt, this famous portrait has had various titles, none of which can be substantiated with any conviction. It gives us a *vivid sense of knowing two people who died nearly two thousand years ago and conveys the intimacy of their relationship with startling realism.*

9

Masaccio to Tintoretto and Veronese, who in the course of barely two centuries produced a range of masterpieces which are the very foundation of our visual aesthetic experience. This achievement in painting, architecture and sculpture was paralleled by similar, though not so spectacular, achievements in the sciences and humanities.

Throughout Italian art, from Cimabue to Tiepolo there are certain consistent characteristics, some at least of which can be traced back to the remote past. Partially defended from the rest of Europe by the Alps and the Dolomites, divided throughout its length by various mountain ranges, exposed throughout most of its length to sea-borne perils which could come from Africa, from Greece, from the Slavonic lands of the East, and from the peoples of the North, Italy's emergence as a national and cultural unity is one of the miracles of history. Even its ethnic mix is remarkable. Around 1000 BC when immigrants from Bohemia and Hungary imported that iron-age culture which was to derive its name from one of its most spectacular sites, Villanova near Bologna, the peninsula was divided among a whole host of different tribes, of whom the most famous were the Samnites, the Ligurians, the Messapians, the Sabines, the Volscians, the Latins and the Etruscans. Echoes of these primitive, racial diversities were to persist long after they had ceased to have any political significance or conscious influence, and they may be seen as the ultimate source of that rich, regional diversity which was to be one of the most fruitful stimulants of Italian art throughout the centuries.

It is significant that one of the most culturally active, and for a long time politically successful, of these tribes was the Etruscans whose name is perpetuated in Tuscany, the part of Italy which was to be productive of so much great art from the thirteenth century onwards. A piratical, bloodthirsty people, of unknown origin, the Etruscans had remarkably inquisitive and acquisitive aesthetic impulses, seizing from whatever cultures – Greek, African, Syrian, Assyrian – they contacted in their explorative depredations, those things which corresponded most closely to their own spontaneous, dynamic creative style. Endowed with a taste for complicated and elaborate ornament, complex linear patterns, and religious fantasies of a mystical kind, they also had a passion for the subtle, accurate and realistic depiction of human beings. Despite the conventional smile which appears on the faces of so many Etruscan sculptures – and which may, possibly rather fancifully, be thought of as the remote prototype of that on the Mona Lisa – they possess a very real sense of actual portraiture. The main cause of this remarkable verism was religious; the Etruscans believed that when a dead man was portrayed on his tomb, his personal features should be immediately recognizable to the gods who came to collect his spirit. Both explorative and traditional, Etruscan art still preserves its enigmas, made all the more incomprehensible because their Indo-European language was for long not fully understood.

But, the mystery of Etruscan culture was compounded by its almost total disappearance as a vital force, and the movement of political power southwards. Rome, strategically placed on its hills at the lowest crossing point of the Tiber, linking the two areas of the fertile coastal plane, Etruscan on the north, Latin on the south, had become a city by 575 BC when the marshy cemetery was laid out as a forum. Speaking a language remarkable for its clarity and precision, the Latins laid the foundation of their power by evolving a legal system unlike anything known in the world before, one which still underpins the law of many twentieth-century countries. Regulating their internal problems with this system, the Romans began the gradual, but remorseless conquest of all the neighbouring tribes, accompanying it, as they were to persist in doing throughout their subsequent history, by an elaborate system of colonization. By 260 BC Roman rule had spread over about 50,000 square miles (129,500 sq km); the peoples absorbed by it were made into Roman citizens, who paid direct taxes; allies supplied men for its armies, and the combination of the Latin language and Roman law made Italy the springboard for further conquests. But, this was not achieved without

2. Reclining figure from an Etruscan sarcophagus
Baked clay, 25 × 35 in (63 × 88 cm)
Museo Gregoriano Etrusco, Rome

Typical of the Etruscan tradition of funerary art, this figure, dating from about the fourth century BC reveals those aspects of realism combined with formal decorative patterns, which were to leave a lasting imprint on Italian art.

difficulties. Marauding bands of Gauls from the north were a frequent threat to the very existence of Rome for more than a century, and then there was the most serious threat of all from Carthage. The Carthaginian armies had defeated the legions time and time again until Scipio Africanus finally annihilated Carthage in 202 BC. But, even these trials were not without their cultural compensations. The Gauls, who eventually became respectable Roman citizens, introduced interesting artistic elements – abstract, lively and rhythmical – from their surviving bronze age culture. The Punic Wars brought Roman soldiers into contact with other cultures, especially Greek, and this was reinforced when in the course of their imperialist expansion they annexed Macedonia, the Greek city states, and the Hellenistic kingdoms in Asia Minor, Syria and Egypt. The links between southern Italy and the Hellenistic culture had always been close, and indeed that part of the country was generally known as *Magna Graecia* or Great Greece.

The Roman army had become a unique reservoir for the pooling of human experience, and although Rome had not released any new productive activity, it had organized what was virtually a world economy in a remarkable way. There was a brisk sea trade with India, and eventually regular imports of such things as parrots, silks, drugs and even dancing girls from as far away as China. Roman imports were paid for in textiles, glass, pottery ware and coral, with the adverse balance being made up in golden coins, later found as far afield as Ceylon, Iceland and China. The expansion of urban civilization which Rome created concentrated the resources of newly conquered lands in the hands of politically minded businessmen, the *equites*, who formed joint-stock companies which farmed taxes for the state, and eventually moved into the aristrocracy. Julius Caesar, Brutus and even Cicero all belonged to this class.

Consumed with a passion for conquest transferred into actuality by the fighting quality of its legions, by the administrative skills with which its civil servants ruled the peoples under its subjugation, and by the engineering genius which created a network of communications which reached from the confines of India to the borders of Wales and Scotland, Rome had become by the beginning of the Christian era not only the capital of an Empire, but the treasure house of the world. Roman conquering generals brought back to the city spoils which were both symbols of imperial power, and of personal prestige. By the time of the Empire the Romans had become art-collectors on a massive scale, and the artistic treasures they accumulated or created were to make their city a repository of styles and images which would be drawn on time and time again throughout the centuries to revitalize the artistic language of Europe.

Although Roman collectors accumulated works of art from many places, including Egypt, their main predilection was for Greek sculpture of the Hellenistic period. Looting took place on a massive scale. Five hundred bronze statues were taken away from Delphi alone, and a whole quarter of Rome, in the neighbourhood of the Villa Publica, was given over to the sale of works of art, many of them, according to Suetonius and other writers, forgeries. During the reign of Hadrian it became common practice to inscribe statues with signatures of the great artists of the past.

The extent to which the Romans had developed a taste for the niceties of art collecting can be deduced from the fact that we still know the names of the owners of masterpieces which now adorn the museums and art galleries of Europe. Sulla, the first of the great soldier-collectors, owned the *Hercules* of Lysippus; Julius Caesar acquired the *Head of Jupiter*, now in the Louvre in Paris,[1] the statue of *Meleager* in the Vatican Gallery and the lovely *Venus* now in the Hermitage in Leningrad. The huge figure of *Melpomone* in the Louvre, and the bronze *Hercules* acquired in the nineteenth century by Pope Pius IX for the Vatican adorned the theatre which Pompey built for himself on the Janiculum, and the gardens of Sallust on the Quirinal contained such famous pieces as *The Dying Gaul* and the *Venus and Cupid* now in the Belvedere of the Vatican. Young Romans went treasure-hunting in Greece and Asia Minor in the same way that in the eighteenth century English noblemen went on the Grand Tour. Their tastes were clearly defined, and a letter which Pliny the Younger wrote to his friend Annius Severus in AD 102 suggests the standards expected of the artists of their own time as well as of the past:

'I have just bought a Corinthian bronze statue. It is small, but pleasing, and finely executed, at least if I have any taste, however defective my judgement in these matters, as in others probably is. However, I think that even I have enough taste to discover the beauties of this figure, and as it is naked, any faults which may exist, as well as the perfections are more observable. It represents an old man in a standing posture. The bones, the muscles, the veins and the wrinkles are so

3

4

strongly expressed that the figure seems to be alive. The hair is thin and scanty, the forehead broad, the face shrivelled, the throat lank, the arms languid, the breast fallen and the stomach sunk, and the back view gives the same impression of old age. It appears to be a genuine antique, both because of the tarnish, and from what remains of the original colour of the bronze. In short, it is a performance so highly finished as to attract the attention of any art lover and delight the most ignorant spectator. This induced me, a mere novice in art appreciation, to buy it. But, I did so, not with any intent on placing it in my own house, but with putting it in some conspicuous place in my native province, preferably in the temple of Jupiter, for it is a present well worthy of a temple and a god. Pray thee do this small commission for me. Give immediate orders for a pedestal to be made. I leave the choice of marble to you, but let my name be engraven upon it, and, if you think proper, my titles'.[2]

There could be few more revealing sidelights on the world of Roman art: the concern with personal prestige, tempered by a desire to make objects of artistic value available in the public domain; the respect for Greek art, a respect which often spilled over into actual imitation, and, most revealing of all, the emphasis on vivid realism which Pliny saw as the touchstone of artistic excellence. It has become a truism of art history that this sense of realism is one of the hallmarks of Roman art, and the quality which most sharply differentiated it from the Hellenistic prototypes which it imitated. This was to be an enduring characteristic which was to outlive the Roman Empire. A comparison between portraits in sculpture or painting produced in the first few centuries of our era and those being produced by Italian artists five hundred years later show a continuity of tradition; it is also possible to see that the Hellenistic passion for dramatic movement and technical virtuousity which informs *Eros and a Dolphin* or *The Drunken Silenus* is very much the same as that which inspired Bernini's *The Rape of Proserpina*. The concern for the validity of visual appearances and for psychological verism about which Pliny is so revealing, was a basic characteristic of the Italian artistic tradition for more than a millenium. The ultimate sources of this are varied and complex. On the one hand there was the Etruscan tradition which, in the pre-Christian era, had evolved representational skills unequalled in any other culture of the time. Then there was the religious tradition, which encouraged aristocratic Roman families to preserve images of their ancestors. Hellenistic art itself had been showing tendencies in the same direction, even before they were so emphasized by the Romans, and right up to the fourth century AD there were alternating waves of emphasis on either the realistic or the ideal, often dictated by the taste of different emperors. Claudius (10 BC–AD 54) favoured the native Roman taste, Nero (AD 37–AD 68) with his inherent romantic tendencies started a move towards exuberant Hellenistic idealism; a reaction to dry realism set in under Vespasian (AD 9–AD 79) and persisted until the reign of Hadrian (AD 76–AD 138), when a more emotional approach became apparent; figures are often bearded, and the eyes are incised, with the pupils drilled or even, in the case of metal statues, filled with different material to give a more highly dramatic effect.

This ambivalence about imitating the Greeks or being true to a more native tradition was reflected in the attitude the Romans adopted towards artists and the status they occupied in society. The passion for collecting works of art of the past, tended towards a marked depreciation of contemporary artists, even though, often enough they had been imported from Greece to make replicas of works from their homeland. Usually they were slaves – though the word should not be understood in quite the menial sense which it has acquired in subsequent centuries: 'tied household servants' might be a more accurate phrase. 'We offer prayers and sacrifices before the statues of the gods, but we despise the men who make them'[3] wrote Seneca, and the physical exertion required in the creation of sculpture helped to maintain the menial position of those who made it. Even when the artist was a free man, his wages were low, and were arrived at by deducting the cost of his board and lodging. A craftsman working in stucco was paid the same wage as a bricklayer or baker; a mosaic worker was paid according to the area he covered each day. Bronze statues were valued according to their weight, and with

5

5. *Eros and a Dolphin*
Marble, 64 in (164 cm)
Farnese Collection, Museo Nazionale, Naples

Although much restored, this group, with its incredible technical virtuosity and its complex compositional rhythms, presents the kind of sculptural tour de force *which five* centuries later would be the hallmark of the creative genius of artists such as Bernini. Friezes showing Eros at play were common in Pompeii and in later Roman art.

the introduction of highly organized foundries and workshops, they were produced on a large scale and the price fell quite dramatically from the time of Nero onwards. This tendency to mass-production had marked artistic effects. The technical abilities which had been so highly prized in the early days of the Empire were superseded by a search for more speciously dazzling effects. Drills were used more frequently, and a concern with creating smoothly polished surfaces supplanted the earlier precision of modelling and the delight in pure craftsmanship. Stock bodies were frequently made, to which different faces could be attached, and these were often changed, either for reasons of economy, or to celebrate changes in the régime.

With painting the situation was somewhat different. Although it never achieved the status reached by poetry, the regard in which it was held improved as time went by. Nero, Hadrian and Alexander Severus were all amateur painters, and their example was followed by many Romans of the upper classes, who were prepared to pay quite highly for slaves to teach them art. Even so, painting was only considered socially respectable as long as it was not practised for gain.

As a result of a series of natural accidents, our knowledge of Roman painting is far more extensive than that of any other culture. In AD 79 the towns of Herculaneum, Pompeii and Stabiae were buried beneath an eruption of Vesuvius, and were thus preserved in their original state to await the attention of the enthusiastic archaeologists of the eighteenth century, who revealed their treasures to an enthralled world. The wealth and luxurious self-indulgence of the Roman ruling classes were reflected in the villas which they built for themselves – Cicero had no less than eighteen in different parts of Italy – and which they not only decorated with statues, but covered with a wealth of mural paintings. As with Roman sculpture, this showed a division of loyalty between respect for Hellenistic precedents – less easily distinguishable because of the almost complete disappearance of classical Greek painting – and the expression of Italian attitudes and traditions. One of the most famous of these murals, the *Aldobrandini Wedding*, so called because it was discovered on the Esquiline Hill in 1604 under the papacy of Pope Clement VIII whose family name was Aldobrandini – had been accessible before the excavation of the Vesuvian towns, and was copied by numerous artists such as Van Dyck, Rubens, Pietro da Cortona and Poussin, and helped to create the image of classical painting which became an integral part of the European tradition.

In contrast to the few paintings such as this which have survived from the city of Rome, the wall paintings of Herculaneum, Pompeii and Stabiae were created for families which were, though rich, less exalted in the social hierachy – provincials rather than cosmopolitans. When first they were discovered, and indeed for more than a century afterwards, they were despised by critics. In the late twentieth century, however, they have come to be appreciated more. Not only do they possess a strong sense of poetic realism, which can be seen even in stock mythological scenes and representations of religious rituals, often marked by a strong emphasis on minor details – such as the disarray of a hair style, or the presence of some domestic animal – but they breathe a sense of spontaneity, which was not to be seen again in European art for another five centuries. Many of them depict landscape in a style which seems to foreshadow the work of Salvator Rosa and other artists of the seventeenth century.

Pliny attributes the popularization of landscape as a suitable subject for the

6. The Aldobrandini Wedding
Detail of a fresco, 36 × 95 in (92 × 242 cm)
Vatican Library, Rome

Painted on the walls of a Roman house and discovered in 1605, the Aldobrandini Wedding *was, until the discovery of the Vesuvian towns, the only significant piece of Roman painting known to European artists. It is easy to understand why its effect was so powerful, and to see the extent to which in its impressive modelling, vivid realism and sophisticated composition it is an epitome of all Italian painting. The complete picture represents a wedding banquet and has been copied by many painters, principally Rubens, Poussin and Van Dyck.*

6

7

7. *Landscape with Buildings and a Bridge*
Fresco, 9 × 13 in (23 × 34 cm)
Museo Nazionale, Naples

There is more than a suggestion here of one of those *seventeenth century. The poetic quality is matched by the*
landscapes which Poussin was to make famous in the *marvellous realization of space.*

decoration of villas to a Roman painter of the time of Augustus, known variously as Ludius, Studius or Statius, but it would seem that they had been used as a background to mythological scenes for some time before then, and had probably been derived from Greek sources. In these paintings there is a certain degree of stylization; rustic scenes with craggy rocks of the kind which feature in fourteenth-century Florentine and Sienese painting, dramatically crooked trees, and picturesque temples which would not have looked out of place in an English eighteenth-century garden. Gradually, however, the landscape element came to predominate, and figures were used largely to give a sense of movement and vitality. That illusionistic element, which was always to remain a persistent ideal in the Italian visual idiom, and which was to be one of its dominant elements from the fourteenth century onwards, was largely encouraged by the actual structure of the houses for which these works were executed.

The typical Roman house was based on a rectangular plan. A vestibule led through a narrow passage to a central court or atrium, on either side of which was grouped a selection of bedrooms and living-rooms, varying in complexity and size according to the wealth of the owner, but generally tending to be small and dark. There was, therefore, a need for some form of decoration, and this was to be found in poor and rich homes alike. One of the main functions of these paintings was to expand the sense of space, creating the impression of larger or more sumptuously appointed rooms within or, by presenting landscape vistas, to suggest windows opening out onto the countryside. This feeling for nature was alien to the Greeks, but was particularly important to the Italians and was destined to become part of their tradition. Throughout Roman painting runs a delight in nature, which can vary in its expression from large landscapes with atmospheric effects, rapid and impressionistic in execution, (which seem not to decorate the walls on which they have been painted, but to dissolve them away by the use of sophisticated perspective) to minutely observed, accurately recorded images of trees and shrubs, flowers, birds, rabbits, snakes and hens. Stemming partly from the generally accepted view that an artist could best display his virtuosity by creating pictures which could deceive the eye of the spectator, this development of an art form which came to be one of the accepted branches of painting – still-life – became in the hands of these Roman artists as important as portraiture. These works are marked by imaginative vigour, by a freshness of vision, and by an ability to comprehend in one complex composition a whole host of disparate elements. Their popularity was clearly well-established, and they were sometimes translated into mosaic. So too were those fresh, often satirical, scenes of daily life which were to be found either in private houses or on the walls of shops and public buildings. People playing games, wandering musicians, market and street scenes, tavern interiors and representations of plays on the comic stage bear witness to that hunger for recording reality which typifies the whole art of Rome; but in these instances it is flavoured with a suggestion of satire or burlesque, anticipating the development of caricature which was to become a recognized art form in seventeenth-century Italy.

There is indeed something to be said for the notion that Roman painting as exemplified in its survivals from Pompeii was basically divided into formal and popular categories. Generally, formal art was a repertory of motifs, themes and styles which was selected according to contemporary artistic taste to suit the religious, philosophical or literary tastes of a socially ambitious patron. Predominant in the field of formal art were those religious and mythological scenes which conveyed to those who saw them a very clear message, usually meant to explain something about the owner of the house to which they belonged – that he was an initiate of the mysteries of Aphrodite, Adonis, or Dionysus, or that he belonged to some particular sect. Much of these meanings are now lost to us, and the subjects may very well have occasionally been chosen as a way of 'keeping-up with the neighbours'. On the other hand, those series of scenes which adorn The Hall of the Mysteries at Pompeii are clearly connected with some ritual ceremony – in this case, as all the participants are women, the only male figure being that of a small boy, probably a preparation rite for a wedding. Sometimes, when the figure of a deity appears, it is probably because the house was under the protection of that particular god or goddess.

Popular art on the other hand, simple, direct, sometimes naive, was concerned with day-to-day things – fruit, flowers, fish, street scenes – and operated on a simpler, more direct level of human taste and experience. The precision of observation and the vitality of form to be found in these works made a unique contribution to classical art of an especially Italian kind. Often they were depicted in mosaic – that most lasting of pictorial media – with the same stylistic characteristics as mural painting. Some of these mosaic pictures were made in the studio within a tray-like frame, in fine tesserae, for use as the central panel of a larger, less delicate pavement, and even moved from one such site to another. A whole group of these mosaics is concerned with fish and other fauna, and may possibly be from the same workshop. Examples in this chapter show fish which are depicted so realistically that they can be identified, in almost all cases, with species still to be found in the Bay of Naples. Among the more familiar are eel, prawn, octopus, squid, lobster, bass, red mullet, dogfish and a murex shell.

The painted portraits which have survived are as realistic as their sculptural equivalents, and are remarkably similar to the Egyptian mummy portraits of the same period. Probably the most famous is that of a man and a woman, sometimes described as a baker and his wife, because it was found in a house at Pompeii which had an adjoining area containing bread or patisserie ovens. It has also been suggested that it is a portrait of Paquius Proculus, a local politician, whose election poster was found on the outside of the house. Whoever the couple may be, they have been portrayed with a striking psychological veracity, and their faces are remarkably similar to types which one would find in late twentieth-century Italy. The man is holding a papyrus roll with a red seal, which may be a commission, and the woman holds to her lips a stylus for writing on the two-leaved wooden diptych, coated with wax, which is in her right hand. It would be tempting to suggest that all these accessories point to some literary connotations, but there are other portraits of young women also holding writing tablets and styluses, so it may have been no more than a pictorial convention of the time.

To compare the ancient *Primavera* shown in this chapter with Botticelli's version of the same subject is to realize the extent to which in the first century of our era Italian artists were showing characteristics of style and technique which were to keep recurring throughout the centuries. This is especially apparent in the mastery of perspective which the artists of Pompeii achieved. Although they had not discovered that scientific form which involves a single vanishing point, and which was to be the great revelation of the late fourteenth century, they combined various types of perspective, often in the same painting, to achieve remarkable spatial effects. With these they evolved a form of interior decoration, often brilliantly conceived, which confirmed the Italian tendency of concentrating on the interior of a building rather than on its exterior. This was to be a precedent which formed the foundation of the flowering of Renaissance mural art. It may well be that many of these paintings and mosaics were produced in imitation of Greek prototypes, which have been subsequently lost, and some at least must have been done by immigrant Greek artists. There still remains in all of them, however, a special local flavour.

8. Marine Fauna
Mosaic, $4\frac{1}{4} \times 4\frac{1}{4}$ in (11×11 cm)
Museo Nazionale, Naples

Precision of observation in this mosaic is matched by the skill with which the artist has been able to present the actual movement of the fishes as they swim through the water.

Practically all the fauna in this work from Pompeii are still to be found in the Bay of Naples, ancient Rome's first window on the Mediterranean.

9

10

22

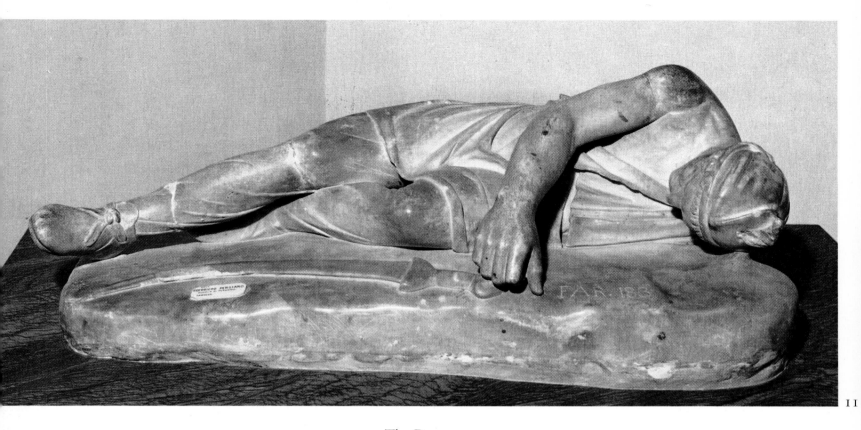

9. The Dancer
Bronze, 60 in (150 cm)
Museo Nazionale, Naples

Although this is the traditional title of the work, with the implicit suggestion that the woman is engaged in some ritualistic dance, the position of her right arm might suggest that she was carrying something on her head. It is highly *possible that this piece together with several similar examples from the Villa dei Pisoni, Herculaneum, are copies of a much older Greek series dating back to the fifth century BC.*

10. Artemis of the Ephesians
Alabaster and bronze, 81 in (203 cm)
Farnese Collection, Museo Nazionale, Naples

Goddess of nature, Artemis was one of the main deities of Ephesus, and her cult spread to southern Italy in the first century BC. This strange, hieratic figure is very remote from *the humanistic verism of Italian art, though the fine quality of the workmanship suggests that it was probably made by native craftsmen.*

11. A Dead Persian
Marble, 38 in (96 cm)
Farnese Collection, Museo Nazionale, Naples

In the period between 283 and 133 BC a whole series of statues were produced at Pergamum, of which this is one, showing dead barbarians – Persians, Gauls and Amazons. *This particular example clearly belongs to that group. The sense of the abandonment of death is strikingly conveyed by the long flowing lines of the composition.*

12

12. *Pan and a Faun*
Marble, 62 in (158 cm)
Farnese Collection, Museo Nazionale, Naples

The story represented by this technically sophisticated group is that of Pan, the pipe-player, teaching his skills to the young god Apollo (an alternative theory is that the teacher is the centaur Chiron and the pupil Achilles). The *counterpoint of the composition and the look of dedicated but apprehensive concentration on Apollo's face give the work an almost Baroque feeling typical of the work of the great seventeenth-century sculptor, Gian Lorenzo Bernini.*

13. *Hermes in Repose*
Bronze, 41 in (105 cm)
Museo Nazionale, Naples

Probably based on a Greek prototype by Lysippus, this remarkable work, depicting the messenger of the gods at rest, shows the extent to which a sculptor can convey a sense of respite not only in the face, but throughout the whole body.

14. *The Farnese Bull*
Marble, 137 in (350 cm)
Farnese Collection, Museo Nazionale, Naples

The punishment of Dirce, Queen of Thebes, who was tied to the horns of a mad bull, was one of the more popular themes of Hellenistic art, demanding as it did considerable technical ingenuity and skill. The most famous version, of which this is a copy made c200 BC, was according to Pliny, a work in bronze, executed by two Greek artists.

15. *The Farnese Hercules*
Marble, 124 in (317 cm)
Farnese Collection, Museo Nazionale, Naples

Taken from the Baths of Caracalla, Rome, this gigantic work was to be a source of inspiration to sculptors of the sixteenth and seventeenth centuries. It reveals an unusual aspect of Hercules; not triumphant, but dispirited after his seduction by Omphale. It was probably copied in Greece for a Roman patron.

16. *Apollo Belvedere*
Marble, 88 in (224 cm)
Musei Vaticani, Rome

This heroic figure of Apollo takes its name from the castle of Belvedere in Rome where it has been housed since its discovery in the early sixteenth century. It is in fact an unusually fine Roman copy of a fourth-century work, which was responsible for the creation of that idealizing naturalism which we associate with the greatest Hellenistic sculpture. Praxiteles had pioneered an entirely new tradition of softly modelled figures which renounce the stern frontal poses of the earlier 'kouros' tradition. It is recorded that the sculptor Lysippus even worked from plaster casts taken from life. The tree trunk is probably the copyist's later invention and the fig leaf, of course, is modern.

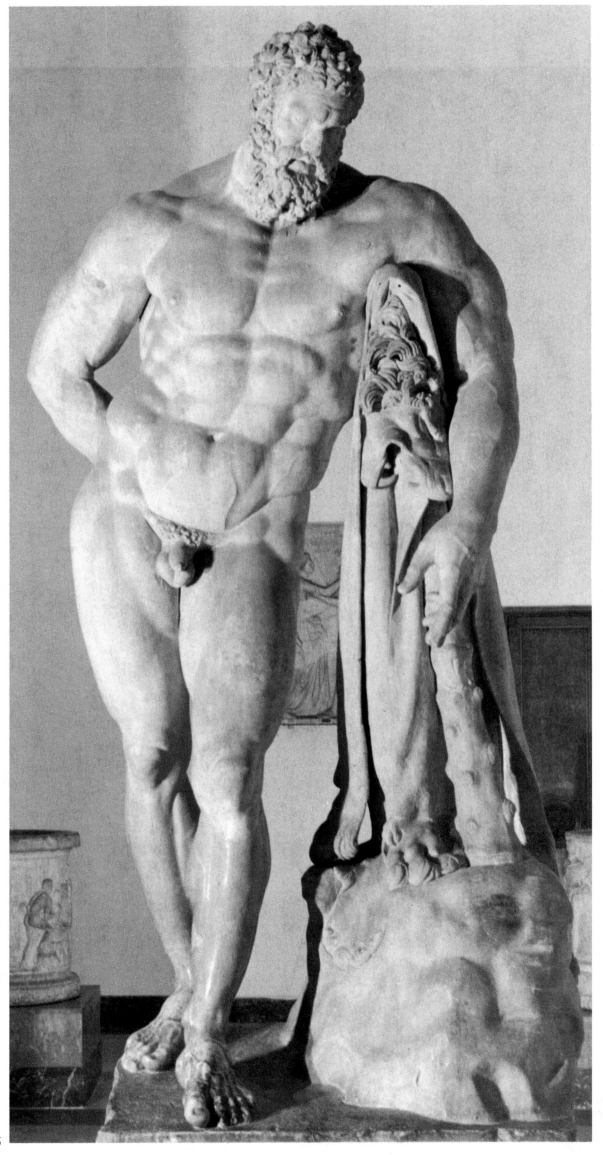

15

17

17. *Aphrodite Genetrix*
Marble, 69 in (176 cm)
Museo Nazionale, Naples

Regarded by Julius Caesar as the protective goddess of his family, Venus in the guise of mother, or producer of life, was to become one of the classic themes of Italian iconography, transformed later into Holy Mother Church, or the Virgin Mother. The Greek original was probably of the fifth century BC.

18. *The Belvedere Torso*
Marble, 62 in (159 cm)
Pio-Clementino Museum, Rome

Dating from the first century BC, this remarkable fragment had a great influence on many artists of the High Renaissance. This is to be seen with especial clarity in *Michelangelo's figures on the ceiling of the Sistine Chapel. It is signed by the Athenian sculptor Apollonius, son of Nestor, who worked in Rome in the late Republic.*

19

19. *The Laocoön*
Marble, 95¼ in (242 cm)
Pio-Clementino Museum, Rome

Discovered in 1506 in the ruins of the Baths of Titus, Rome, this work was immediately recognized as that described by Pliny the Elder as the work of the Rhodian sculptors Athenadoros, Agesander and Polydorus. Pope Julius II had *it placed in the orange groves of the Belvedere Palace in a niche designed by Bramante, and it not only inspired Raphael and Michelangelo, but became an inspiration to the exuberant dynamism of the Baroque movement.*

20. *Woman's Head*
Marble, 70 in (180 cm)
Museo Nazionale, Naples

The studied simplicity and formal grace of this bust from Herculaneum is allied to a remarkable sense of perception. *The modelling of the hair style is especially sensitive and there is little idealization in the woman's features.*

21. *Head of Antinous*
Marble, 78 in (200 cm)
Farnese Collection, Museo Nazionale, Naples

The favourite of the Emperor Hadrian, Antinous was mysteriously drowned in the Nile in AD 130. After his death he was deified by Hadrian, who founded the city of Antinoöpolis on the site of the fatal incident. Antinous was considered a paragon of beauty and was one of the most *popular subjects in art during the Emperor's reign, and indeed for some time afterwards, often under the guise of Adonis or Dionysus. The untroubled clarity of the face is emphasized by the decorative, stylistic exuberance of his luxuriantly curling hair.*

22

22. Theseus and the Minotaur
Fresco, 35 × 31¾ in (90 × 81 cm)
Museo Nazionale, Naples

This frieze, which shows the grateful Thebans welcoming Theseus after he has slain the monster, is remarkable both for the ingenuity of the composition and the rendering of the naked human body. It is especially interesting to note that whereas a Greek artist of an earlier period would have shown the hero's face as placidly triumphant, here there is a feeling of actual portraiture. Theseus had comparatively little impact as a subject for Renaissance artists.

23

24

25

23. *Head of Socrates*
Marble, $76\frac{1}{4}$ in (194 cm)
Farnese Collection, Museo Nazionale, Naples

It is recorded that the sculptor Lykourgos produced heads of Aeschylus, Sophocles and Socrates for the theatre at Athens in the first half of the fourth century BC, and we can safely assume that this is a Roman copy after the Greek original. Whilst as a portrait the bust undoubtedly conveys an actual likeness to this the greatest of all classical philosophers, we should note the stylized handling of the beard, and a generalization of the features which places Socrates, in the Roman imagination, within the Pantheon of divinity. His ugliness was often mentioned by his contemporaries.

24. *Achilles and Briseides*
Detail of a fresco, $49\frac{3}{4} \times 47\frac{3}{4}$ in (127×122 cm)
Museo Nazionale, Naples

The dramatic intensity of this opening scene of the Iliad, as Achilles sits outside his tent, is enhanced by the antithesis between his gesture and that of Patroclus. Briseides and the soldiers, who form such a dramatic frieze in the background, are dressed in costume which must have been contemporary with the artist who painted the scene.

25. *Portrait of a Girl* (known as *Meditation*)
Fresco, $11\frac{1}{2}$ in (29 cm) in diameter
Museo Nazionale, Naples

It has become, for some reason, an accepted convention in Pompeian painting to portray young girls in this attitude, with a stylus lifted to their mouth and a writing tablet in their hand. The delicacy of the net on her hair and the fine articulation of the hands reveal an artist of consummate skill and perception.

26. *View of a Port*
Fresco, $9\frac{3}{4} \times 9\frac{1}{2}$ in (25 × 24 cm)
Museo Nazionale, Naples

This view of an unidentified port is suggestive of an approach to landscape art which was to remain consistent throughout much of the history of Italian painting. It is extraordinary how the artist conveys space and light.

27

27. Still-life with Peaches
Fresco, $13\frac{3}{4} \times 32\frac{1}{2}$ in (35×83 cm)
Museo Nazionale, Naples

Rooted in popular tradition, and bearing witness both to a deep love of nature and a concern with the ordinary things of life, paintings such as these were not to be seen again in European art for another fourteen hundred years. The perspective and the spontaneity of the arrangement reinforce each other.

28. Still-life with a Bowl of Fruit
Fresco, $27\frac{1}{2} \times 42\frac{1}{4}$ in (70×108 cm)
Museo Nazionale, Naples

This attractive wall-painting was found in the House of Giulia Felice, Pompeii. The iridescence of the glass bowl containing the mixed fruit is complemented by the glowing texture of the grapes and the pomegranate and apple which have fallen out. An unbleached, linen bag probably contains honey. The rustic pot is brimming over with grapes.

29. Fight between Ureus and the Ibis
Detail of a fresco
Museo Nazionale, Naples

Despite the almost monochromatic treatment of this theme, which is Egyptian in inspiration, the sense of drama and hostility is conveyed with an extraordinarily vivid effect. The ibis's enemy is Ureus, the mythological Pharoah's hat.

28

29

30. *Primavera*
Fresco, $15\frac{1}{4} \times 12\frac{1}{2}$ in (39×32 cm)
Museo Nazionale, Naples

The fresh charm of this girl gathering spring flowers, with which she fills the basket held in her left arm, seems to anticipate the delicate fantasies of Botticelli and the Florentine artists of the fifteenth century. The sense of grace is enhanced by the light movement of her dress, and the way in which her fingers grasp the stem of the flower.

31. *The Battle of Issus*
Mosaic, 134×232 in (342×592 cm)
Museo Nazionale, Naples

The most magnificent two-dimensional work of art surviving from Antiquity, and based on an earlier Greek work of the fourth century BC, this mosaic was part of the pavement in the House of the Faun in Pompeii. Its local significance stems from the fact that it represents Alexander the Great defeating the Persians under Darius III at the battle of Issus in Sicily in 333 BC. Surprisingly enough, this subject did not often feature in post-Renaissance art.

32. *Part of a Frieze with Festoons and a Mask*
Detail of a mosaic, 19×110 in (49×280 cm)
Museo Nazionale, Naples

This decorative mosaic shows the deep interest the citizens of Pompeii had in the theatre, where the wearing of masks was essential to the ritual. The subject could well be snake-haired Medusa, one of three monstrous mythological sisters.

32

33. *The Fortune-Teller*
Mosaic, 17 × 14 in (45 × 36 cm)
Museo Nazionale, Naples

Two women, both of them expressing alarm, listen to an old female fortune-teller seated at a circular table, covered with the impedimenta of her profession. Realistic and slightly satirical, this Pompeian mosaic may represent a scene from a play, but it is completely faithful to ordinary life in its vivid execution.

34. *Wandering Musicians*
Mosaic, 19 × 18 in (48 × 46 cm)
Museo Nazionale, Naples

Signed in the top left-hand corner by the artist, Dioscurides *represents one of the most original and lively aspects of the*
of Samos, this life-like representation of a street scene *tradition of popular art so special to Italy at this time.*

35

35. *Achilles and Chiron*
Fresco, 48½ × 46 in (124 × 118 cm)
Museo Nazionale, Naples

The monumentality which was later to mark the work of Masaccio and Piero della Francesca is clearly evident in this first-century work from Herculaneum based on a famous statuary group described by Pliny which was sited on the Saepta Julia in Rome. The theme of a young man and his mentor was a familiar one, though sometimes the two figures were given different names. Chiron was one of the centaurs and the teacher of other heroes such as Jason and Asclepius.

36

36. Funeral Dance
Fresco, $20\frac{3}{4} \times 29$ in $(53 \times 74$ cm)
Museo Nazionale, Naples

Discovered in 1883 in the ancient necropolis of Ruvo, the frieze, of which this is part, consists of thirty-six women dancing in slow processions from left to right, their hands joined. It is a remarkable survival, dating back to the second half of the fifth century BC, and shows clearly how strong Greek influence was in the south of Italy. Wall painting was the most highly valued of all the arts in Antiquity, although due to its extreme fragility we know least about it. This fresco depicting a funeral dance belongs to a type which was widely distributed throughout the Mediterranean world in the fifth century. Although there is no attempt to create the illusion of volume through tonal modelling, a high degree of naturalism has been achieved, and the loose folds of the dancers' robes have clearly abandoned the severe formalism of earlier more highly conventionalized styles of representation. In the drawing of the women's heads we can observe for the first time a profile eye in a profile face, whilst the figures are recognizably individualized. Space is dealt with summarily, using broad bands of background colour, as in most contemporary vase painting, or simply by leaving the pale ground of the plaster itself – a frequent practice. The
Ruvo frescoes provide evidence of the widespread Hellenism in Italian culture after the Persian invasions of the Greek mainland. Such tomb paintings suggest a highly ritualized society flourishing in the south of Italy. Ancestor worship was a fundamental aspect of Italian and Etruscan religion in a strongly patriarchal society. Hence the construction of necropoli, or cities constructed entirely for the dead, at Ruvo and elsewhere throughout the mainland on the outskirts of all major cities and towns. The shape of the individual tomb approximated to the occupant's original house, just as the necropolis as a whole approximated to his or her home town. Painted tombs in Italy constitute only a small proportion of the tombs discovered and excavated and must therefore be directly representative of the urban aristocracy. We may thus think of the dancers as members of the dead aristocrat's immediate family or household. In such funeral art the sacred dance came last in a long sequence of valedictory ceremonies; at the end of those rites which were believed to guarantee the dead person's access to the next world. The paintings are recognized as one of the greatest monuments of ancient Italian civilization.

37. *The Knucklebone Players*
Panel, $17 \times 15\frac{3}{4}$ in (42×40 cm)
Museo Nazionale, Naples

This decorative panel was painted on marble and signed by a painter from Athens called Alexander. The goddess Latana is shown being reconciled to Niobe, who had claimed to be her equal. The reconciliation was not successful, however, and Niobe's daughters are seen playing with knuckle bones, serenely unaware that soon they both will be killed and turned into stone. The work is more or less a faithful copy of a Greek original dating from the fifth century BC. This may be seen from the powerful overall linear design, the delicate drawing of the individual women's heads, and the complete renunciation of contemporary Roman naturalistic modelling. As in most Greek painting, the ground is left to suggest space. The entire emphasis is on the relationship of the figures. Such paintings on marble, of which at least two survive from the city of Herculaneum, were probably intended to fit into the centre of a surrounding wall decoration. The style of the panel reflects the continuing influence of Hellenistic culture in Roman society, and may be seen as analogous to the copying of Renaissance paintings for later stately homes.

II

Heaven on Earth

THE ADVENT OF Christianity did not immediately alter the nature of art in Italy until the edict of Milan, promulgated by Emperor Constantine the Great, in AD 313. In its early stage it was largely a hidden religion, not apparently different from those other mystery sects, whose beliefs in rituals were recorded on the houses of Pompeii and Herculaneum. Christian artists adopted the iconography of Greece and Rome to depict, in a symbolic way, their own beliefs. The early images of Christ – young and unbearded – made him appear as a kind of Apollo. However, once Christianity became not only a tolerated, but an official religion, the scene changed. Triumphal paintings and mosaics filled the new basilicas with episodes from the Old and New Testaments; a whole new iconography came into existence which was to dominate western art for fifteen hundred years. The cult of saints – often transformed versions of local pagan deities – and the whole liturgy of the church with its emphasis on magnificence and splendour, provided new incentives to artistic activity. It created a need for objects, chalices, reliquaries, monstrances, croziers and the like, which had not existed in classical times. The importance attached to the word, in the form of Bibles, breviaries and missals, also brought with it another new outlet for the exercize of the pictorial imagination, especially after vellum had taken over from papyrus, providing a more malleable surface and greater durability, thus facilitating the transmission of artistic ideas between widely different centres.

For more than two centuries the city of Ravenna, with its marvellous mosaics in the Mausoleum of Galla Placidia, and the churches of S. Apollinare Nuovo, S. Apollinare in Classe and S. Vitale, was to be the virtual capital of the country, looking towards Byzantium and creating pictorial patterns which were to dominate Italian art until the Renaissance. In that other centre of the same tradition, Venice, a permanent mosaic workshop was established for the decoration of the Basilica of San Marco, which was to become important for the future of Venetian painting.

More important, however, than the survival of Graeco-Roman traditions was the influx of new peoples into Italy between the fourth and ninth centuries. In this period a great bubbling over of the cauldron of central Asia took place, which sent hordes of barbarian tribes west into Europe under the pressure of those even more savage than themselves. Vandals, Goths, Huns, Visigoths and Lombards swept down from the north, and the turmoil of Italy was only quietened when Charlemagne was crowned

1. CIMABUE (c.1240–c.1302)
The Madonna in Majesty
Panel, 181 × 103½ in (460 × 263 cm)
Uffizi, Florence

Although the Byzantine influence is still clearly strong, it is possible to see in this work, painted for the church of Santa Trinita in Florence, those qualities of monumentality and *brilliant composition which justify Vasari's statement that Cimabue, 'gave the first light to the art of painting'. It is probably a late work.*

48

I

49

Emperor by Pope Leo III on Christmas Day 800. Alas, even that peace was largely deceptive. In the south constant raids from the Moslems of Spain and Africa took place, and by AD 902 Saracen rule was established throughout Sicily. This was only terminated in the eleventh century by Norman invaders, and the misfortunes of the south were further complicated by marauding bands of savage Magyars.

It is all too obvious why this period has been described as the Dark Ages. But, on the other hand, all these new additions to the cultural meld of Italy were to lay the foundations of a brilliant future. Geographically, politically and culturally, it had become a divided land, each of its main components possessing its own creative traditions which were grafted onto the Graeco-Roman and Byzantine background which was common to them all. For the next five centuries, these differing strains would interact on each other to produce a kind of creative ferment with ever-changing stylistic mixtures and cross-fertilizations, out of which the finest achievements of Italian art would grow. In the north around Milan the influence of the Holy Roman Empire, with its Carolingian background, predominated. In the north-east, Venice was the centre of a Byzantine area which stretched to Padua and Verona in the west, and to the borders of Greece in the east. Here too, there were strong oriental influences stemming from the republic's ever-increasing trade with the Far East. Pisa developed its own contacts with non-European sources, whereas Florence remained true to its Etrusco-Roman past, emphasizing a certain purity and formalism as well as a concern with design all of which were apparent, for instance, in the church of S. Miniato built in the eleventh century. In the far south, Norman, Byzantine, Greek and Arabic influences produced a creative compost out of which grew one of the finest flowerings of medieval culture during the reign of the Emperor Frederick II whose court was the centre of artistic pursuits and activities which were to anticipate the Renaissance by two centuries. Rome, battered by waves of conquerors, its churches falling into disrepair, its monuments pillaged to construct homes for its inhabitants, presented a less positive picture of artistic activity, although the mosaic work of the Cosmati family represented a vital local tradition. It was only as time went on, when the triumph of the Popes over the Emperors became a reality, that the papacy was to emerge as one of the richest, most influential powers in the peninsula. But, although its potential as one of the greatest art patrons of all time became apparent, the actuality was delayed by the schism which for most of the fourteenth century ensured that there were rival claimants to the See of Peter at Rome and Avignon.

If the barbarian invasions and their aftermath had destroyed a great deal of the actual physical structure of classical civilization, Christianity brought about a change in man's attitude to the universe and to the nature of his own experience which deeply altered the art he produced. Transcendental in nature, medieval Christianity saw the world and man merely as reflections of a divine order of things; its outlook was conceptual rather than perceptual, and the realism of the classical world was replaced by a hieratic formalism. The effects of this attitude were reinforced by the basically abstract nature of those barbarian art forms, which had been absorbed into the mainstream of Italian culture as a consequence of the invasions during the Dark Ages. Figures began to lose their definition and their objective relationship to each other; perspective gradually disappeared; images became mystical objects to be worshipped and adorned with incrustations of gold and gems. They were not representations of reality, but reality itself.

By the thirteenth century, Italy had become a cultural battleground, struggling between Byzantine influences, renewed as a consequence of the Crusades and various native tendencies and complicated by the influx of French Gothic art. The latter had been introduced by the great religious orders such as the Cistercians as well as by the French conquest of Sicily and the south by Charles of Anjou. At the same time, however, it was becoming a land of wealth, and this, perhaps more than anything else, stimulated the arts. Venice had achieved a commanding position as the great trading link between Europe and the East; Genoa, Pisa and other coastal cities gained an economic primacy which stimulated the growth of a money market. Italian merchants began to dominate European trade and, while the northern nations wasted their energies on the Crusades and internecine struggles, the natives of Florence, Siena and other cities became rich on trade with the East and the West. Fine cloths were exported to Africa and the East to pay for luxuries, and sold to the rest of Europe for gold. Industry became combined with commerce, and by the beginning of the thirteenth century, Florence was producing around 100,000 pieces of cloth, and the customs dues paid in the port of Genoa quadrupled between 1274 and 1293. Venetian and Genoese convoys departed on a regular basis to the ports of Flanders and England. Italian businessmen such as the Frescobaldi, the Peruzzi and, richest and most famous of all, the Medici dominated the financial worlds of England, France and the Low Countries. The heraldic device of the Medici – golden balls – is still used by pawnbrokers today as the symbol of their trade.

The growth of cities and city states, the political structure of which could alter from place to place, and from time to time according to the varying historical climate, but all of which contained a financial oligarchy of one kind or another, stimulated the division of labour, and fostered professionalism in the arts and crafts as well as elsewhere. The guild system became a dominant factor of economic life, and painters came to be associated with the Guild of St. Luke, which also included doctors and pigment dealers. Artists' guilds laid down rules of conduct and professional practice, and refusal to join met with social ostracism as well as exclusion from all sources of patronage. They also offered their members a great deal of support, giving loans and even sick pay. Anyone who wished to become an artist started off as an apprentice (often the profession of artist was a family calling, and this tendency continued until at least the eighteenth century), and then could do one of two things. Either he could work for hire by the year, month or day in the workshop of one who was already a master; in 1339, for instance, Jacopo di Donato in Florence contracted to work in a shop which produced clothes chests with painted scenes on them for twelve florins a year (the wages of an unskilled labourer were about the same). Alternatively, a young artist could rent a *bottega* – a shop built into the lower part of a house – and set himself up as a master.

As the demand for paintings grew these *bottege* became more complex in structure – more like small factories – and those run by artists such as Giotto Orcagna and Bernardo Daddi in Florence were both large and popular, a fact which makes precise attributions very difficult. It has recently been suggested, for instance, that the only known works actually signed by Giotto were not his own and that he put his name on them to prove that they had come from his workshop, despite the fact that the handling of the paint was clearly not his own. Many artists might spend their time painting details in works which were sold under the name of their master.

This division of labour was especially apparent in the making of mural paintings. First of all the master would make a charcoal sketch of the complete work roughed out on a layer of plaster. Then he would go over it in red earth with a brush to fill out the general design. The whole sketch was then divided up into sections, each of which would take a day to complete. These sections were completed in the time allotted, while the plaster was still wet, and details were added later *a secco*, that is to say, when the plaster was dry. These co-operative schemes imposed unity on a conception, but also they demanded personal skill, imagination and administrative flair on the part of the master who directed them.

It was the combination of great demand and increasingly complicated techniques of production which gave birth to the first great individual names in pre-Renaissance art. But there were also other factors. French influence had become increasingly apparent in the thirteenth century, largely because of the intellectually progressive Cistercians, who built important abbeys in Lombardy, Tuscany and the south, and this had encouraged the growth of North Gothic forms of decoration. At the same time the capture of Constantinople by the participants in the Fourth Crusade had brought newly invigorated Byzantine influences into Italy. These two currents came together in the flowering of Franciscan art which took place in honour of the vastly popular cult of St. Francis at Assisi, the centre of the order at the end of the thirteenth century. The first name to be associated with this was that of Cimabue, a rather shadowy figure, despite the fact that he is mentioned by Dante in *The Divine Comedy* (Purgatory XI, 94–6) and that, as the teacher of Giotto, he has been credited with the paternity of European post-medieval painting. Although it is recognized that he owed a great deal to the received Byzantine tradition, Cimabue's paintings have a plastic monumentality and note of grandeur which he may well have acquired from contact with Roman artists such as the mosaicists Torriti and Pietro Cavallini who were restoring early Christian art in St. Peter's during the late thirteenth century, and whose own productions reflected classical influences.

A number of frescoes in the Upper Church at Assisi are attributed to Cimabue, and they show the same dramatic intensity, the same concentration on the face as a vehicle of expressive emotion and the same decorative linear rhythms as the Uffizi *Madonna*. But even Dante's reference to him hinges on the fact that he was overshadowed by his pupil Giotto and posterity has confirmed the judgment. Born in Florence *c.*1267, Giotto became a member of the Painters' Guild there in 1311, and the city was to remain the centre of his active life, although he also worked in Rome, Naples (where he became court painter to Robert of Anjou), Padua and Milan. A man of many interests, both artistic and commercial, he was the first artistic personality to emerge clearly as a figure of individual distinction since classical times. In his *Decameron*, written in the middle of the fourteenth century, Boccaccio said of him:

> 'He had a mind of such excellence that there was nothing given by Nature, the mother and mover, together with the continuous movements of the sky, of all things, which he with stylus, brush or pen, could not paint with such realism, that it seemed not so much a representation of a thing, but the real actuality, so that often in his paintings, mens' eyes were deceived. He brought back to life that art which for many centuries had been buried under the error of those who in painting had sought to give pleasure to the eyes of the ignorant rather than delight the minds of the wise. It is, therefore, with justice that he may be called one of the lights of Florentine glory'.[1]

The comment is significant, for it includes at least three examples of a new attitude towards art which was to become increasingly important. The first is the emphasis on realism as a standard for the judgment of works of art; the second is that simplistic notion, which was to dominate aesthetic thinking for the next five centuries, that cultural history proceeds in a simple line of direct progress, and the third is that there are two arts, one for 'the ignorant', the other for 'the wise'. Equally important too, is the notion that an artist can achieve personal and professional distinction. He need no longer be one of the 'rude mechanicals', and in the case of Giotto this attitude receives further support from Petrarch's will in which he bequeathed to the Lord of Padua:

> 'My picture, or icon, of the blessed Virgin Mary, the work of the distinguished painter Giotto, given to me by my friend Michele Vanni of Florence, whose beauty amazes the masters of the art, though the ignorant cannot understand it.'[2]

2. GIOTTO (*c.*1267–1337)
The Madonna in Majesty
Panel, 129$\frac{3}{4}$ × 80$\frac{1}{4}$ in (325 × 204 cm)
Uffizi, Florence

The extent to which Giotto introduced into art a new sense of form, a brilliance in modelling and a keener sense of visual reality, is apparent in this detail from a painting commissioned for the church of All Saints in Florence. The influence of the revolutionary and widely emulated sculpture of Nicola Pisano is evident in the rendering of volume.

2

This personal fame was fully justified. Giotto was the first to explore the scientific representation of the visible world and expand its means of expression. He depicted the human figure in all its actions in a manner which had not been seen since Roman times, and for the Byzantine emphasis on formal brilliance and decorative elegance he substituted truth to the realities of personal experience. Although his most famous work is the fresco cycle which he painted on the wall of the Scrovegni Chapel in Padua, he was closely associated with the cycle of the life of Saint Francis in the basilica at Assisi, and produced frescoes in St. Peter's and St. John Lateran in Rome. He established a repertoire of gestures and positions, a narrative style, and a grammar of expression which became accepted for another century or more. His immediate followers were numerous, although few achieved his sense of monumentality and moral earnestness. Some pupils such as Bernardo Daddi introduced a strikingly picturesque note and a lyricism, which were to predominate until the middle of the fourteenth century when a reversal to more austere Byzantine modes of expression was pioneered by Orcagna (c.1308–1368), whose real name was Andrea di Cione, and who was not only a painter, but a sculptor and a master builder. Giotto's career established Florence as the centre of a style which influenced all Italy in varying degrees, less perceptibly in Venice, more interestingly in Siena, where Duccio, though he kept his style within the Byzantine framework, introduced a freshness of feeling, a sense of dramatic narrative, a tenderness which was to be one of the hallmarks of the art of the City of St. Catherine. He is also noted for his passionately splendid colours.

The fame achieved within their own lifetimes by painters such as Cimabue, Giotto and Duccio, no less than the attitude to them and their productions evinced by the reactions of Petrarch and Boccaccio, are indicative of a new social and economic climate for painting and sculpture, which eventually was to help change their very nature.

By the fourteenth century, paintings had become an accepted marketable commodity, and the transactions of the wily, bargain-driving Francesco di Marco Datini, the merchant of Prato, whose life and transactions have been revealed by Iris Origo in her fascinating book *The Merchant of Prato*, were typical of those many Italian textile dealers who were art-dealers on the side. His main outlet was through Avignon, which he frequently visited, and from whence he would write back to his partners with specific orders. In September 1373 he ordered:

> 'A panel of Our Lady, with gold background, two doors and a pedestal, with decoration and leaves finely worked into the frame. It must be imposing with fine and beautiful figures by the best master who lives there (Florence), and with lots of figures. In the middle there should be either Our Lord on the cross, or Our Lady according to what you find. It really must be very good, the most beautiful you can get, though it must not cost more than six florins.'[3]

(Some idea of the value of a florin then may be deduced from the fact that the annual salary of a working man in Florence was about fourteen, and that the annual average profit of the Florentine branch of the Medici bank between 1397 and 1420 was about 1,100 florins.) In the following year one of his partners wrote to him from Avignon:

> 'You say you can't find pictures at the price we want, because there aren't any going so cheap. In that case if you can't find works which are cheap, leave them. They're not much in demand here anyway. You should only buy them when the artist is hard up. So if you're looking round and find a master who's in need of money, then do a deal with him. Of the five panels which Andrea bought, we've sold three. We took ten florins each, making a very good profit on the transaction. If the master he got them from should have any fine, good panels costing four, five or six florins – if they are fine and cheap – you should take one or two, but no more. Those with good figures sell well here; ugly things don't go at all.'[4]

Nor was art-dealing of this type confined to Italian outlets. It was probably through

3

3. BERNARDO DADDI (*c.*1290–1350)
The Meeting of St. Joachim and St. Anne at the
Golden Gate of Jerusalem
Detail of a polyptych
Uffizi, Florence

This is the side panel of a larger painting depicting St.   *Virgin Mary conveys Daddi's sense of poetic rhythm,*
Pancras. This account of the meeting of the parents of the   *delicate colouring and skilful massing of volume.*

55

some member of the Datini family that Abbot Thomas of St. Albans (1349–96) was able to take back to England from Italy a large panel painting for the high altar of his monastry, and at about the same time, the painter Tomasso da Modena executed a set of panels for the Emperor Charles IV, which were placed in the church of St. Catherine at Karlštejn in Bohemia. The paintings which the Datini and their like sold to French merchants at Avignon did not stay there, but spread throughout France and probably beyond. Jean, Duc de Berry (1340–1416) was a great collector of Italian things – paintings and tapestries from Florence; cameos, coins and medals from Rome; manuscripts from Padua and Venice. The traffic was not only one way. French ivories, enamels and tapestries, works of art from the court of Burgundy, alabaster statues from Nottingham and examples of *opus Anglicanum* – the famous embroidered liturgical vestments made in English nunneries – were among the more noticeable imports from outside Italy. Throughout the fourteenth and fifteenth centuries there were close links with Flemish painting too. The Neapolitan humanist Fazio (*c.*1430) placed Jan van Eyck among the most illustrious men of his time, and Cardinal Albergati, who was sent to Bruges by the Pope in 1431, sat for him for his portrait which survives only in the form of a drawing in the Albertina, Vienna. The contacts of Hans Memling (1430–94) were closer. Among his patrons were Italians such as Tomasso Portinari, the agent for the Medici bank in Bruges, whom he painted with his wife (the work is now in the Metropolitan Museum of Art in New York) and also produced the portrait of their son Benedict. Other Flemish artists whose works were greatly sought after in Italy were Hugo van der Goes, who was commissioned by Portinari between 1476 and 1478 to paint a triptych for the church of Sant' Egidio in Florence which created a sensation when it arrived there, and exercized considerable influence on the work of Filippino Lippi, Ghirlandaio and Lorenzo di Credi and may even have attracted the attention of Leonardo. The taste for Flemish art was to persist long after the fifteenth century. In 1666, Cardinal Carlo de' Medici bought the famous *Deposition from the Cross* by Roger van der Weyden, which was already in Italy, and quite apart from artists such as Rubens and Jan Lys who had Italian connections, later Medici collected works by Rembrandt, Jan Steen and Schalken, and employed painters like Sustermans to paint their portraits.

This new cosmopolitanism, which had become apparent by the 1360s, could in one sense be seen as a by-product of a dominant money-economy, and certainly owed a great deal to the financial acumen and far-flung contacts of Italian merchants and financiers, producing that style which dominated the more advanced forms of European art – miniatures, illuminated manuscripts, tapestries, and embroideries, as well as paintings between about 1350 and 1425, and which since the end of the nineteenth century has been known as International Gothic. The style spread from France, Italy and the Low Countries through Germany, Bohemia, England and Spain. Uniting the Flemish feeling for realism and the aristocratic refinement and elegance which evolved in the courts of France and Burgundy, with the lyrical naturalism, the taste for the antique and the passion for nature which were becoming characteristic of Italian art, International Gothic was marked by a new interest in secular, mythological and bucolic subjects. Enamoured of rich, luxuriantly vivid colours, linear arabesques of movement and complicated patterns of composition, it has affinities with later art movements such as Mannerism and, more recently, Art Nouveau, which are equally obsessed by the exotic, even the bizarre. In Siena, it first became manifest in the work of

4. HANS MEMLING (*c.*1433–94)
Portrait of a Young Man
Panel, $12\frac{1}{2} \times 6\frac{1}{2}$ in (26×20 cm)
Gallerie dell' Accademia, Venice

This sensitive and deceptively simple portrait of an unknown youth, suggests the influence which the paintings of Northern Europe were to have on sophisticated fifteenth-century Italian artists and patrons.

4

5

5. SIMONE MARTINI (c. 1284–1344)
The Annunciation
Panel, $124 \times 148\frac{3}{4}$ in (315×378 cm)
Uffizi, Florence

Probably the finest painting produced by the Sienese school of the fourteenth century, this magnificently decorative work combines the cursive elegance of the Gothic tradition with a new awareness of feeling and emotion. This is shown especially in the shyness of the Virgin Mary and the urgency of expression on the face of the kneeling angel.

artists such as Simone Martini who grafted onto the traditions of Byzantine richness, which he had inherited from painters such as Duccio, a sinuosity and sweetness which are emphasized by the expressiveness of his colours and even by a certain angularity which seems to partake of the essence of the Gothic spirit. Another aspect of this new spirit was especially apparent in the works of Ambrogio and Pietro Lorenzetti which are marked by a sense of vivid realism, acute social observation – apparent not only in their scenes of Sienese life, but even in their religious paintings – and passion for nature. It has been suggested that the great fresco *Good and Bad Government*, which Ambrogio painted for the town hall of his native city, is the first great landscape in Italian painting, and Sienese artists of his generation often achieved effects of perspective which Florentine artists were not to attain for another century. It was in the north, however, that the Italian dialect of International Gothic reached its height, in the works of painters such as Stefano da Venezia and above all Gentile da Fabriano. The latter's *Adoration of the Magi* typifies all that is most enchanting about the style; the sense of decorative exuberance, the warm, lively colours – foreshadowing what was to become a familiar Venetian quality, the skilful perspective, the host of exciting happenings which are taking place in the background, the birds, horses and dogs, the use of a canopy to give depth and spatial richness to the picture and the acute observation of the characters. The entire *oeuvre* has a fairy-tale like atmosphere which characterizes so much work of this particular episode in the evolution of Italian painting.

Styles were already beginning to travel more rapidly from centre to centre as artists were becoming more peripatetic. Simone Martini worked in Naples for Robert of Anjou, and in Avignon – where he painted the frontispiece to Petrarch's copy of Virgil – for the papal court, and possibly the Datini. Lorenzo Monaco carried the style from Siena to Florence. Gentile da Fabriano went from Verona to Venice to paint frescoes in the Doge's palace (completed by his pupil Pisanello, and since destroyed), then on to Florence, where he painted *The Adoration of the Magi* for the chapel of Palla Strozzi in S. Trinita, moved on to Siena and Orvieto, and ended up in Rome executing frescoes for the Lateran Basilica. These latter were completed by Pisanello, who had also started off in Verona, travelled extensively in northern Italy and worked in Naples. At the same time, however, older styles survived, and everywhere there were artists who, though still deeply embedded in the Byzantine tradition, picked up details from new styles to give their works an air of modernity.

6

7

6. DUCCIO DI BUONINSEGNA (*c.*1255–*c.*1315)
Madonna Rucellai
Panel, 177 × 114 in (450 × 290 cm)
Uffizi, Florence

Painted towards the end of the thirteenth century, Duccio's majestic Madonna Rucellai was in all probability originally the central panel of a large polyptych which was later dismantled. It is a perfect example of Duccio's humanizing approach to the impassive conventions of Byzantine painting. The hem of the Virgin's robe reveals that love of abstract decoration which was so strong a feature
of Duccio's art, and which guaranteed the survival of a linear decorative tradition in Sienese paintings long after the artists in nearby Florence had developed a more thorough-going naturalism. Duccio has successfully reconciled the naturalism of Giotto and his immediate followers to the more traditional taste of his Sienese patrons and it is strange to note that Vasari once ascribed this picture to Cimabue.

7. GIOTTO (*c.*1267–1337)
The Madonna in Majesty
Detail of a panel, 128 × 80½ in (325 × 204 cm)
Uffizi, Florence

Painted a little after the major fresco sequence in the Arena Chapel at Padua c1310, Giotto's Maestà conforms to the Medieval model of depicting the Virgin and Child enthroned. This detail shows the heads of various saints and
angels gathered around the Virgin's throne. The carefully observed modelling reveals the full extent of Giotto's radically innovative introduction of naturalism into Medieval art.

8

9

8. GHERARDO STARNINA
(c.1354–c1413)
The Thebaid
Panel, $83\frac{3}{4} \times 37\frac{1}{2}$ in (213 × 96 cm)
Uffizi, Florence

The desert of Thebes was considered to have been the source of monasticism, and the lives of its hermits became a popular theme at a time when the Franciscans and Dominicans were making a great impact on society. This ambitious landscape is the work of an artist who is reputed to have been the teacher of Paolo Uccello.

9. AGNOLO GADDI (c1333–96)
The Crucifixion
Panel, $22\frac{1}{2} \times 30\frac{1}{4}$ in (57 × 77 cm)
Uffizi, Florence

Brought up in the tradition of Giotto, Agnolo Gaddi's cool pale colours, vital rhythms and vivid presentation anticipate by a decade or more the achievements of the masters of the International Gothic style. Agnolo was the son of Taddeo Gaddi, who had been Giotto's favourite and most able pupil. This Crucifixion scene exemplifies the dominant tendency in Florentine painting in the second half of the fourteenth century. The various incidents in the story of the Crucifixion are combined in a single moment of pictorial time, in the manner of Medieval painting. The flat, decorative treatment of this crowded scene, together with the uniformly gilded sky, shows how Giotto's followers retained his general facial naturalism at the expense of his concern with the convincing illusion of three-dimensional space. Agnolo Gaddi was the teacher of Cennini, author of the earliest Italian book on painting.

10

11

10. GENTILE DA FABRIANO (1370–1427)
St. Nicholas Saving a Ship at Sea
Panel, 14¾ × 25 in (38 × 64 cm)
Musei Vaticanni, Rome

In the 1420s Gentile was called to Rome to work for Pope Martin V and it is probable that this panel dates from that period. Lacking something of the splendour of the painting of The Adoration of the Magi, *it demonstrates the artist's ability to achieve a sense of narrative unity and compositional fluency.*

11. GENTILE DA FABRIANO
The Adoration of the Magi
Panel, 142¾ × 126½ in (364 × 323 cm)
Uffizi, Florence

The brightly decorative colours, vivid details (note especially the procession winding its way up the hill in the background) and acute sense of social observation discernible in the faces and dress of the attendants, make this probably the most important Italian contribution to the International Gothic *style. Seen in closer detail, the painting reveals the mastery of precise brushwork which Gentile commanded, no less than the remarkable feeling for the texture of objects. In a way the work seems to reflect something of the new wealth.*

12. LORENZO MONACO (c.1370–c1425)
Scene from the Life of St. Benedict
Panel detail
Uffizi, Florence

Though born in Siena, Lorenzo spent all his working life in Florence, but as this work suggests, he never lost something of the spirit of his birth-place. A miniaturist by training, *who illuminated several manuscripts, something of the luminous colouring and sinuous lines of that art form are to be seen in his panel and altarpieces.*

13

13. PIETRO LORENZETTI (*fl.*1320–48)
The Madonna in Glory
Panel, 51 × 21 in (145 × 122 cm)
Uffizi, Florence

Lorenzetti, together with his brother, Ambrogio, were *show an affinity with the naturalistic forms of the*
painters working in the Sienese tradition whose panels *revolutionary sculptor Giovanni Pisano.*

14

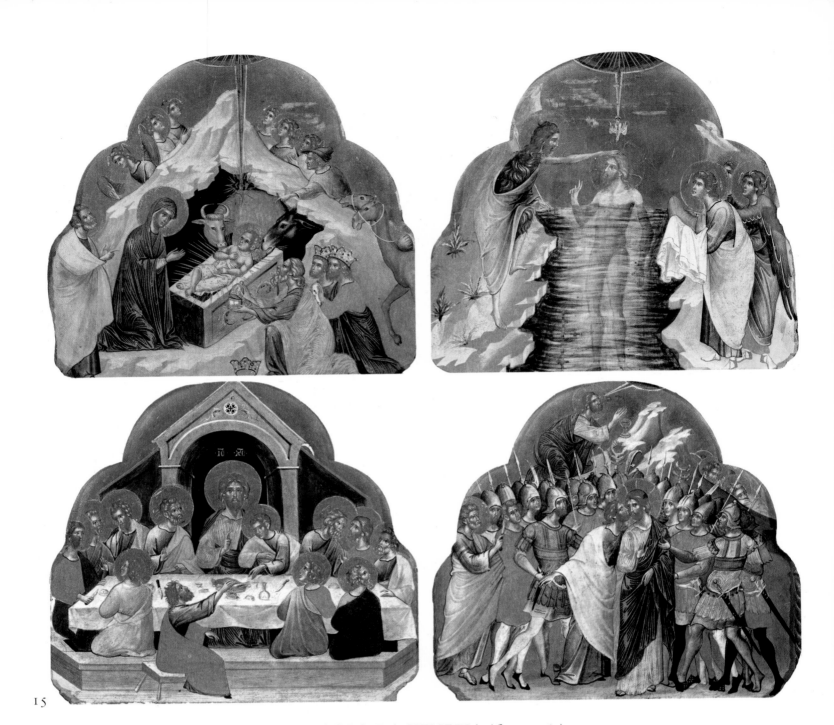

15

14. PAOLO DA VENEZIA (fl.1333–62)
The Madonna and Child Enthroned
Panel, 36¾ × 35 in (142 × 90 cm)
Gallerie dell' Accademia, Venice

Some idea of the difference between work executed in Siena and Venice at this time can be got by comparing the works of Paolo da Venezia with his contemporaries. Venezia's work is still embedded deep in the icon traditions of Byzantium and the influence of the mosaics of San Marco is very apparent.

15. PAOLO DA VENEZIA
Scenes from the Life of Christ
Panel each 15¾ × 35 in (40 × 90 cm)
Gallerie dell' Accademia, Venice

In comparison with Venezia's The Madonna and Child Enthroned, *a new sense of observed reality is apparent here, due possibly to the influence of Giotto. This is to be* found especially in the figure of Christ in the Baptism scene. These four panels were part of a larger painting, The Coronation of the Virgin.

16

17

16. STEFANO DA VENEZIA (*fl.*1360–85)
The Coronation of the Virgin
Panel, 28 × 21 in (71 × 54 cm)
Gallerie dell' Accademia, Venice

Despite the Gothic–Byzantine quality of this panel, evident especially in the pose of the Virgin, and the treatment of the haloes, there are already signs of a new spirit *abroad – in the often atmospheric colouring and in the loving attention paid to the details of the wide variety of musical instruments.*

17. JACOBELLO DEL FIORE (*fl.*1400–39)
The Coronation of the Virgin in Heaven
Panel, 111 × 118 in (283 × 303 cm)
Gallerie dell' Accademia, Venice

Painted for the cathedral of Ceneda in 1438 this remarkable work is still formally embedded in Medieval tradition, with its emphatic architectural structure and the Byzantine *quality of many of the figures. On the other hand, it shows an exceptional talent for the narrative handling of a complex and spectacularly crowded subject.*

18. LORENZO VENEZIANO (*fl.*1356–72)
The Mystic Marriage of St. Catherine
Panel, 37½ × 22¾ in (95 × 58 cm)
Gallerie dell' Accademia, Venice

Although traditional Venetian attitudes are apparent in this painting, which reflects the wide impact of the cult of St. Catherine of Siena, the fact that the angels and indeed the *Holy Infant are dressed in contemporary clothes – note especially the shoes of one of the angels on the left – is suggestive of a more immediate awareness of the present.*

19

19. HUGO VAN DER GOES (*c.*1440–82)
The Adoration of the Shepherds
Panel, $99\frac{1}{2} \times 119\frac{1}{2}$ in (253×304 cm)
Uffizi, Florence

Painted at Ghent c1474 for Tomasso Portinari, the
Medici's agent in that city, this panel was moved to Florence
at the beginning of the sixteenth century and placed over the

high altar of the church of Sant'Egidio, where the guild of
painters held their meetings. Its influence on Florentine art
was very significant.

20. ROGER VAN DER WEYDEN
or ROGIER DE LE PASTURE
(*c.*1399–1464)
Deposition from the Cross
Panel, $43\frac{1}{4} \times 37\frac{1}{2}$ in (110×96 cm)
Uffizi, Florence

Roger van der Weyden's Deposition together with Hugo
van der Goes' Portinari Altarpiece, provided fifteenth-
century Italian painters with the most advanced style of
contemporary Flemish oil painting. Working principally
in Brussels, where he was the leading court painter, Roger's

work combined a strong decorative gift with a richly sombre
sense of colour and an extremely intense approach to his
subject matter. The frail body of Christ introduced an
element of pathos into religious art which must have seemed
startlingly convincing.

III

The Triumph of the Eye

OVER THE PAST few decades the familiar concept of the Renaissance has been taken to task. Its very existence has been doubted, its nature critically examined, its antecedents pushed further and further into the past. But whatever historical polemicists may say, no matter to what extent the concept of a 'rebirth' is re-qualified, there can be no doubt that from the first quarter of the fifteenth century to the end of the sixteenth a cultural explosion took place in Europe, which transformed the nature of Western man's outlook on the world, and produced two generations of artists whose works have never been equalled, let alone surpassed, both in quality and quantity. In 1505, for instance, in the city of Florence alone, Leonardo da Vinci and Michelangelo were making the cartoons for the Palazzo della Signoria; Perugino was working on his *Annunciation*, Raphael was painting his *Madonna del Granduca* and among the artists living in or near the city were Botticelli, who was sixty-one years old, Lorenzo di Credi, Fra Bartolommeo, Filippino Lippi and Andrea del Sarto. Pinturicchio was at work in Siena, Bernardo Luini in Milan, Carpaccio, Giorgione, Palma Vecchio and Titian in Venice. The painters, architects and sculptors of the period produced an entirely new kind of art, which became the foundation of European visual culture for more than five centuries, and which even today provides a touchstone, the value of which is proved even by the vehemence of those who reject it. What is even more remarkable is that this phenomenon was basically an Italian one. There were also French, German and even English versions, but, especially in painting, sculpture and architecture, there was nothing which could remotely compare with, for instance, the range of painters which stretched from Giotto to Titian and Veronese

The idea of a 'rebirth' happening goes back to the fifteenth century, when it was used to describe a new passion for the literature of Greece and Rome which had been stimulated by the increasing traffic in ancient manuscripts promoted by the incursions of the Turks into the Byzantine Empire. It was first applied to the world of the arts by Vasari in his book *The Lives of the Most Eminent Painters, Sculptors and Architects*, published in Florence in 1550, and the connexion between literature and art was a very close one. A more widespread knowledge of 'humanistic' literature naturally induced new approaches to art, and the works of Botticelli, for instance, show the extent to which the secular mythology of Greece and Rome, filtered through the writings of fifteenth- and sixteenth-century Italians, provided new sources of inspiration and a whole new range of subject matter.

More significantly, the study of Greek and Roman literature gave new meaning to those works of art from pre-Christian times which so abundantly littered the soil of Italy and which to the men of the earlier Middle Ages had seemed but idols dating back to a remote, pagan past. Ghiberti, the Florentine sculptor, records that in the middle of the fourteenth century a Greek statue of a nude woman supported by a dolphin

I

1. RAFFAELLO SANZIO called
RAPHAEL
Leo X
Panel, $60\frac{1}{2} \times 46\frac{3}{4}$ in $(154 \times 119$ cm)
Uffizi, Florence

The studied simplicity of this composition, in which the Pope is flanked by Cardinals Giulio de' Medici and Luigi de' Rossi, gives a sense of grandeur, balanced by the sharp observation of character and the skill with which the *illuminated manuscript has been painted. Raphael's extreme technical virtuosity guaranteed him a successful career as a portraitist and nowhere is this more apparent than in this direct and yet subtle group portrait.*

2

(possibly Aphrodite) was discovered in Siena. At first the citizens were delighted and not only set it up on a pedestal in the middle of the city, but commissioned Ambrogio Lorenzetti to paint it. Within a short time, however, Siena became involved in its ultimately unsuccessful war with Florence, and one of the more influential citizens suggested that the statue had brought them bad luck. They reburied it therefore – but this time in Florentine territory. Yet within little more than a century, shortly after the discovery of *The Laocoön* in the Baths of Titus in Rome, Machiavelli was writing:

> 'Quite apart from anything else, it really is extraordinary how people pay anything for a mere fragment of ancient statuary, so that they can keep it in their house, and so add dignity to the reputation of their family.'[1]

It is impossible to over-emphasize the passion for classical antiquity which suffused Italy from the fourteenth to the sixteenth centuries. In Rome especially, archaeological fervour reached its heights. The Popes had re-established that city as the sole seat of their power in 1417, after the disasterous Avignon schism and set about enhancing its status.

This fresco in the Vatican is clearly influenced by Raphael's dramatic tableaux of papal scenes. Sixtus is shown at work in the Vatican library, surrounded by prelates and officials, *all of whom are framed and defined by the grandeur of their surroundings. It is not difficult to sense in this painting the reality of contemporary political life in the papal court.*

In the eight years of his pontificate, Nicholas V restored much of the ancient city; fountains were rehabilitated, fallen arches and obelisks re-erected.

Pope Pius II, himself a redoubtable scholar who claimed descent from an ancient Roman family, promulgated a bill forbidding the use of any stone from antique buildings or statues for new constructions, and used a great deal of the immense wealth which accrued to the papacy as a result of the discovery of gold mines on the papal estate at Tolfa, to build up a remarkable collection of ancient works of art, which he left to his native city of Siena. His successor, Pope Paul II, restored the arch of Titus, and started that collection of ancient statues which was later bought by the Medici Cardinal Giuliano, who became Clement VII, and is now in Florence. Sixtus IV opened up the Capitol Museum, and forbade the export of antiquities, and the infamous Roderigo Borgia, Alexander VI, was responsible for the excavations which unearthed the Roman mural paintings known as *The Grotesques*. In 1503, the year of the accession of Julius II, *The Laocoön* was found buried in a vineyard, and was bought by the Pope who, in the previous year, had acquired the *Belvedere Apollo*. The farmer on whose land *The Laocoön* had been found was remunerated by a lucrative position in the papal government, just as several years later the person who found the statue of *Ariadne* was rewarded by being freed from taxes for four years – a formula which was to be of great help in building up the papal collections.

In 1515 Raphael was appointed Superintendent of Antiquities by Leo X, and the Belvedere, together with the Museum of the Capitol, were re-organized and became the finest collection of classical antiquities outside Greece. Cardinal Alessandro Farnese, who became Pope Paul III in 1534, far outstripped any of his predecessors in his zeal for Graeco-Roman art. As a cardinal he had obtained from the previous Pope the right to acquire as many antiquities as he could in one night. He commandeered a fleet of seven hundred ox carts, and stripped the Temple of the Sun in the Colonna Gardens, the Forum of Trajan, the Temple of Neptune and the portico of the Argonauts in the Piazza di Pietra, to lay the foundations of a collection which became the Museo Farnesiano. As Pope his collecting activities continued unabated. From the Gardens of Caesar and the Baths of Diocletian and Caracalla, he brought a whole forest of statues. But he was careful to improve the sites which he excavated, and exposed in the most skilful way as much of ancient Rome as had survived, clearing space around all the most important monuments. Although he left his great collection to the City of Rome, the marriage of his nephew Ottaviano to Margaret of Parma, the daughter of the Emperor Charles V, initiated a century or so of litigation about its ownership, which ended in 1787 when Pope Pius VI, in order not to offend the newly established Bourbon dynasty in Naples, ordered that the collection be moved there, and it is now part of the Museo Nazionale.

The most obvious impact of the interest in Graeco-Roman art was its direct effect on the work of artists, and this was clearly considerable. To enumerate even a tithe of the borrowings is impossible. Both Michelangelo and Raphael owed a clear debt in many of their works to the *Belvedere Apollo*, which appeared also in a book of sketches and drawings in the manner of Ghirlandaio intended as a kind of visual pattern book for artists. Two centuries later, Winckelmann, the influential German historian and critic, was to ensure by his description of it as 'the highest ideal of art among all the works of antiquity' that it would become the male equivalent of the *Venus de Milo*.

But it would be naive to think of the things which took place in the arts in Italy at this time merely as a consequence of the re-discovery of the ancient world. The very quality of life itself had been undergoing changes, often due to simple technical discoveries. The invention of the chimney, which made indoor life more tolerable; the wider use of glazing which took place as cheaper and more expeditious methods of manufacturing glass were discovered; the growing use of public and private baths, introduced from the East as a result of the Crusades; greater sophistication in the production of textiles, were but a few of the things which had been gradually making the struggle for a comfortable existence less arduous. Other discoveries, such as the grinding of lenses, which made sharper vision possible, the improvements in the making of paper and of course, above all else, the invention of printing, which not only facilitated the easier transmission of ideas but also encouraged the use of manuals and similar props to technical dexterity. Improvements in the technique of engraving disseminated imagery more widely and made visual experience more accessible to a larger number of people. These technical developments had been paralleled, especially in Italy, by an expansion of commerce, aided by the introduction of Arabic numerology, and double-entry book-keeping, which put a premium on personal economic initiative and dissolved the last remaining shackles of feudalism. Man was gaining a new confidence in himself. He began to set a higher value on his own personal experience, on his own interpretation of nature, on his own emotional life. This was reflected in a new attitude to the human body, which to medieval man had been the temple of sin and an incitement to evil. Christianity had offered few pretexts for the display of nudity, and as late as the sixteenth century Erasmus still condemned it even in private, as it offended one's guardian angel. But, in Italy the exemplars provided by Graeco-Roman sculpture combined with new hedonistic attitudes to make the naked human figure one of the most important images in art and to find its apotheosis in the works of Michelangelo, Giorgione, Leonardo, Titian, Veronese, Tintoretto and countless others. As Kenneth Clark has put it:

'The nude flourished most exuberantly during the first hundred years of the classical Renaissance, when the new appetite for antique imagery overlapped the medieval habits of symbolism and personification. It seemed then that there was no concept, however sublime, that could not be expressed by the naked body, and no object of use, however trivial, that would not be the better for having been given human shape. At one end of the scale was Michelangelo's *Last Judgement*, at the other door knockers, candelabra, or even handles of knives and forks. To the first it might be objected, and frequently was, that nakedness was unbecoming in a representation of Christ and his saints. This was the view put forward by Paolo Veronese, when he was tried by the Inquisition, for including Germans and drunkards in his picture of the *Marriage at Cana*, to which the Chief Inquisitor gave his immortal reply: "Do you not know that in these figures by Michelangelo there is nothing that is not spiritual – *non vi e cosa se non de spirito?*" and to the second, it might be objected, and frequently is, that the similitude of a naked Venus is not what we need in our hand when we are cutting up our food, or knocking at the door, to which Benvenuto Cellini would have replied that since the human body is the most perfect of all forms, we cannot see it too often.'[2]

Here again the happy accidents of history came to the help of art. Medieval man, when he viewed the human body, did so in a conceptual way; Augustine of Hippo for

3. LUCAS CRANACH THE ELDER
(1472–1553)
Venus and Cupid
Panel, 51½ × 39¾ in (131 × 101 cm)
Galleria Borghese, Rome

A tribute to Cardinal Scipio Borghese's eclectic tastes, this epitome of the northern Gothic nude is a variant on another by Cranach in the Hermitage, Leningrad. Cupid is pointing to a honeycomb which he has extracted from the hollow of the tree, and there is a clear implication of some moral point. Cranach represents a very different ideal of female beauty from that of his Italian contemporaries. Venus appears as the very model of north European chic.

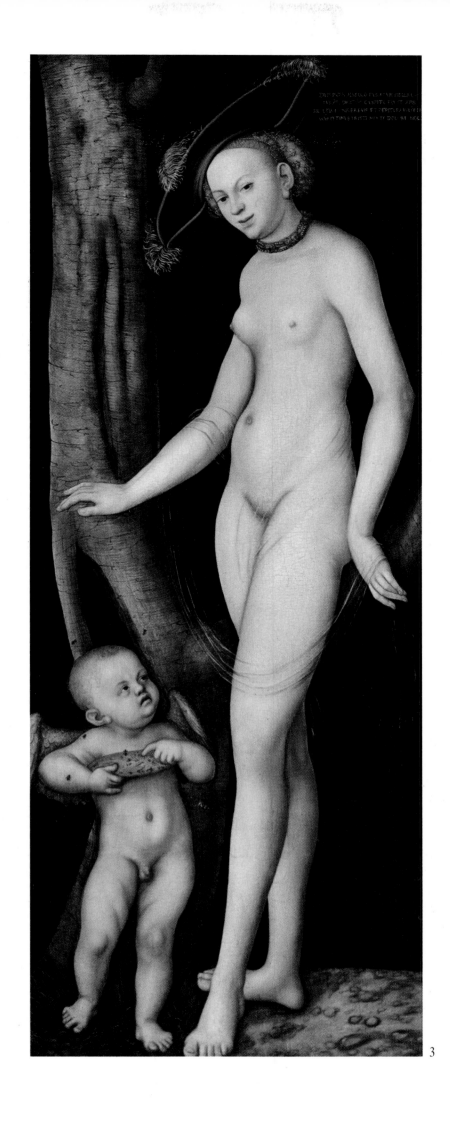

3

4

instance had put forward the view that the numbers which ought to predominate in any analysis of the human body were six and ten, since upon them were based the structure of Noah's ark and Christ's own body. This attitude was reflected in science. The extensive anatomical knowledge possessed by the ancients had been lost when the Alexandrine schools stopped dissecting the human body. Throughout the Middle Ages medical knowledge had been based on the work of Galen and Hippocrates, who had depended on the vivisection of animals, with the result that concepts of human anatomy were based on that of dogs, cats, monkeys and pigs, whose internal organs bore a superficial resemblance to those of human beings.

Gradually, however, as a result of contact with the Arab world, and the development of universities, some of which, Padua being the outstanding example, specialized in medical science, a more empirical attitude, based on the vivisection of human bodies, grew up. This attitude was adopted by artists who were brought into close contact with medical men through their shared patronage of apothecary shops, where both medicaments and pigments were on sale. They also shared the same patron saint, the evangelist, Luke. To represent the human body convincingly, a quite intimate knowledge of anatomy was required and in many cases this was derived not only from the many text books which were becoming available, but from actual vivisections. Luca Signorelli is said to have visited burial grounds to find corpses for his explorations, and Vasari said of Pollaiuolo that 'he understood the nude figure in a more up-to-date way than anyone who had gone before him'.[3] Leonardo was the outstanding example of an artist obsessed with anything in nature which he found susceptible of measurement and analysis. 'Those who are enamoured of practice without science', he wrote in his *Notebooks*, 'are like sailors who go aboard a ship without a rudder and compass never having any certainty of where they go.'[4]

Lorenzo Ghiberti (1378–1455), the creator of the famous bronze doors on the Baptistery of the Duomo in Florence, was only expressing accepted opinion when he said that a painter needed to know grammar, arithmetic, geometry, philosophy, medicine, astrology, history, anatomy and perspective. Piero della Francesca became so enamoured of mathematics that he gave up painting for the last fourteen years of his life to devote himself to its study and wrote a book on painting perspective – *De Prospetiva Pingendi*. This 'divine' perspective which reflects so well two of the main preoccupations of Renaissance man – that of emphasizing the significance of the individual human viewpoint, and that of expressing the belief that the human mind could impose a pattern on all natural phenomena – was one of the dominant elements in Piero's own works; these are lucid, classical exercises in defining space in two dimensions, using infinitely precise lines and cool, subtle colours, which are bathed in an even Tuscan light. It would be long, however, before perspective became an exact science. In fifteenth-century Florence, where it made some of its most spectacular advances, the approach was largely pragmatic, and the credit for discovering certain rules for constructing a picture according to the rules of perspective is attributed to Filippo Brunelleschi (1377–1446) the architect who designed the dome of the cathedral there. His principles had first been put into practice by Masaccio, whose works have that sense of monumentality which he had inherited from Giotto, and which depended so much on that dedication to the discipline of drawing which was to become one of the hallmarks of the Florentine tradition. To some it became an obsession, and of Paolo

4. LEONARDO DA VINCI (1452–1519)
The Annunciation
Detail of a panel, $38\frac{1}{2} \times 85\frac{1}{4}$ in (98 × 217 cm)
Uffizi, Florence

It is in the treatment of the angel that Leonardo's hand is most clearly revealed in this work by the young artist. The detail on the wings, the quick brush-strokes of the foliage and the subtle arrangement of the trees in the background are all typical of his highly individual sweetness and softness of style.

5

Uccello Vasari wrote in his *Lives of the Artists*:

> 'The most captivating and imaginative painter to have lived since Giotto would certainly have
> been Paolo Uccello, if only he had spent as much time on human figures and animals as he spent
> and wasted on the finer points of perspective. He was endowed by nature with a discriminating
> and subtle mind, but he found pleasure only in exploring certain difficult, or rather impossible
> problems of perspective, which, though fanciful and attractive, hindered him so much when he
> came to paint figures, that the older he grew the worse he did them. His wife told people that
> Paolo used to stay up all night in his studio, trying to work out the vanishing points of his
> perspective, and that when she called to him to come to bed, he would say, "Oh, what a lovely
> thing this perspective is".'[5]

The dazzling, almost vertiginous effects which Uccello achieved represented one side of Florentine art, its intellectual rigour. But in the works of painters such as Filippo and Filippino Lippi, Fra Angelico and Botticini, another side of the local tradition became apparent, a feeling for bright, evocative colours, clear light and a lyrical treatment of the subject matter, which contrasted with the spiky, metallic quality of an artist such as Cosimo Tura. Tura came from Ferrara and the quality of his art may well have been the result of local traditions buried deep in the historic past, and these began to differentiate regional styles from each other, as well as to interact with each other to create new and exciting combinations. In the paintings of Luca Signorelli (1441–1523) for instance, who was born in Cortona, but worked in Arezzo, Florence, Rome, Perugia and Orvieto, there is a basic Tuscan quality, reminiscent at times of the figures on Etruscan vases, but superimposed on this, an attitude to reality and to the grotesque which gives his work a remarkable, even brutal, vigour.

The clearest antithesis to the Florentine spirit was that of Venice, where on the foundations of the older Byzantine tradition new and vigorous styles had been growing up, which owed a lot to the city's role as one of the greatest ports in Europe. The Byzantine spirit was responsible for the survival of highly decorative elements, which were often incorporated into local variations on the styles of Giotto or Masaccio, as in the works of Antonio Vivarini and his brother Bartolommeo and Antonio's son Alvise. In the paintings of Bartolommeo the influence of Mantegna, with his heavy dependence on ancient sculpture was apparent, and Antonio worked in collaboration with Giovanni d'Alemagna, a German, to produce works which strongly reflected styles predominant north of the Alps. Such foreign influences were strong, and the Flemish influence was particularly so. Every year convoys of ships went from Venice to the ports of northern Europe, and Flemings had their own quarter in the city, where Venetians must have seen examples of their art. Its influence became especially apparent in the works of Gentile Bellini, with his skills as a portraitist and his ability to record city life in convincing detail and Vittore Carpaccio, with his sense of realism and fantasy, his interest in human detail, and his supremely convincing powers as a master of narrative, so ably displayed in the *Scenes from the Life of St. Ursula* in the Accademia. The nature of Venetian culture, dominated in effect by an oligarchy of rich merchants, preferred realism to idealism, fostered the growth of portraiture, saw art as a means of enhancing social status and promoting civic pride, and yet fostered a romanticism more profound

5. FRA FILIPPO LIPPI (*c*.1406–69)
The Coronation of the Virgin
Detail of a panel, 77 × 112¾ in (196 × 285 cm)
Uffizi, Florence

This painting shows how rapidly Florentine painting had progressed since the time of Masaccio and Fra Angelico on whose styles Lippi's was partly based. This may be seen in the sense of reality and humanity which informs this altar panel painted for the church of S. Ambrogio in Florence. It has been suggested that the kneeling figure in the left corner is a self-portrait. Although the shape of the picture is determined by the Medieval form of the pointed arch, Filippo Lippi creates a single unified pictorial space and employs a consistent light source. Note the lively sense of observation, the feeling that the figures in the painting are actual people and the sophistication of the technique.

6

6. VITTORE CARPACCIO (c.1460–c1523)
The Return of the Ambassadors
Oil on canvas, 117½ × 207½in (297 × 527 cm)
Gallerie dell' Accademia, Venice

The Venetian passion for recording contemporary life in intimate detail, even though it might have a fictitious historical gloss on it, is strikingly exemplified in the urban and domestic details of this episode. This is Italy as the artists of the late fifteenth century would have liked to have seen it; a glorious mixture of archaeology and fantasy, minute detail and social imagination. Carpaccio is thought to have been a pupil of Gentile Bellini.

7. GIOVANNI BELLINI (c.1430–1516)
The Madonna of the Shrubs
Panel, 29 × 22¾ in (74 × 58 cm)
Gallerie dell' Accademia, Venice

A fundamentally private and portable devotional picture, Bellini's Madonna looks back to the firm tonal traditions of Florentine art, while it also exemplifies the expressionistic use of colour which came to dominate Venetian painting in the sixteenth century. Giovanni was the greatest of the Venetian Madonnieri or Madonna painters.

than that experienced by any other city. Some of these qualities had an influence which went far beyond the north east of Italy. The softer side of the Florentine spirit owed much to Domenico Veneziano, credited by Vasari with having introduced oil painting there, and certainly responsible for promoting a new interest in colour and light as essential elements not merely in the decoration, but in the construction of paintings.

It is to the Bellini family, however, that we must look for the formulation of those qualities which throughout the next three centuries would be thought of as typifying Venetian art. Jacopo had been a pupil of Gentile da Fabriano, and was still embedded in the traditions of International Gothic, but Gentile, the elder of his two sons, had spent some time at the court of Mohammed II in Constantinople, where he was exposed to Eastern influences which became perceptible in his paintings. He excelled as a portrait painter – for this again was another new aspect of the economic wealth and interest in the individual which were part of the new intellectual climate – a growing demand for paintings of people, virtually unknown in the Middle Ages. He, like all his family, and

indeed like all his fellow citizens, was passionately devoted to Venice and has left paintings of the life of the city in his time, which manifest a rare ability to deploy large numbers of figures with skill and conviction.

His younger (and probably illegitimate) brother Giovanni, or Giambelline, however, was to be one of the more significant figures in Italian art, encapsulating in his work characteristics which were to become part of the permanent heritage of Venetian painting, giving it a quality immediately recognizable, immediately distinguishable from those of all the other art centres of Italy. Giovanni's works gave colour a new significance in the composition of a painting, blending figures into landscape, and – in opposition to the Florentine tradition – present an image, not of action, but of contemplative lyricism. Probably more than any other artists the Venetians were preoccupied with landscape painting – this is remarkable in view of the fact that their

city was cut off from direct access to nature by the waters of the lagoon. Their continuing interest in the nature and quality of light was equally marked, and the advances which they made in its analysis and depiction during the following century were to influence the whole development of Western painting and to find echoes in the works of Rubens, Turner, Constable, and the Impressionists. Giovanni's own paintings have been seen, in fact, as prototypes of the work of Gauguin. The Flemish influences which still underlay much of the development of Venetian art were more apparent in the work of Antonello da Messina who modelled his portraits on those of painters such as Van Eyck and Memling, but in his larger religious works depended a good deal on the Bellinis. Everything new and vital in the Venetian style was to be found in the work of Giorgione who died of the plague in 1510 at the age of thirty-five. All the lyricism of Giovanni Bellini is associated in his few surviving works with a sense of atmosphere, a poignancy and an ability to blend figures into their natural setting in such a way as to create a harmony reflected in both line and colour. It was he who made possible the evolution of Titian, a figure who was to dominate the art of the republic during most of the sixteenth century.

Art went with riches – all the greatest creative centres of the Renaissance were remarkable for their wealth. But there were differences, which when grafted onto regional, cultural backgrounds diversified still further the rich pattern of Italian painting. Venice, standing apart from the rest of Italy, cool to the papacy, rejecting even the thought of being dominated by a single ruler or family, clung adamantly to the concept of republican virtue and possessed a civic pride which verged on megalomania. The Doge's Palace, which was to become one of the greatest treasure houses of European art, was also one of the largest single sources of commissions for

8. GENTILE BELLINI (*c*.1429–1507)
Procession in St. Mark's Square
Oil on canvas, 114¼ × 293¼ in (367 × 745 cm)
Gallerie dell' Accademia, Venice

St. Mark's Square is much the same today as it was when Gentile Bellini painted it with such clarity at the end of the fifteenth century. The number of precisely observed portraits in the work is no less remarkable than the skill with which he organizes this vast conglomeration of figures. The power and ritualized authority of the Venetian state is stunningly conveyed by his direct central emphasis on St. Mark's, which was the Doge's private chapel.

9. PIERO DELLA FRANCESCA
(*c*.1410/20–92)
Scene from an Allegory
Panel, 18½ × 13 in (47 × 33 cm)
Uffizi, Florence

This and the painter's other scene from an allegory are painted on the back of Battista Sforza's and her husband's portraits. On the back of Federigo's, the Duke is shown seated in a chariot, with an angel holding a wreath over his head. In front are personifications of the Virtues. The serenity of the landscape and the sense of triumphant dignity are reflected in the elegant script below. It was frequent practice to signify the virtues of a patron in emblematic terms on the reverse of a portrait. In Federigo's case, this involved portraying both the Arts of Peace and those of War.

9

painters for more than two centuries. Then there were the various *Scuole* – part guilds, part business associations, part charitable trusts – which commissioned works from almost every artist of repute in the fifteenth and sixteenth centuries; Carpaccio's works for the Scuola di S. Giorgio, Gentile Bellini's for the Scuola di S. Giovanni, Giorgione's for the Fondaco dei Tedeschi, Tintoretto's for the Scuola di San Rocco are but a few of the more famous examples of this kind of patronage. But though they might have been republican in name and even spirit, the great Venetian families were as aristocratic in their tastes as their contemporaries in other Italian cities, who combined wealth with overt political power. The palaces of those whose names were inscribed in that Book of Gold which was the guide to the holders of real power, the Dandoli, the Contarini, the Foscarini, the Vendramin, the Cornari and the Barbari were splendid with works of art. It was a Venetian notary living in Treviso, who in the fourteenth century had produced the first known catalogue of paintings and drawings, and a whole tradition of art collecting had grown up dating back to the Fourth Crusade.

With the exception of ecclesiastical and civic art, the Venetians tended to favour paintings as adornments to their houses, as windows on the world and as documents of the pleasure of life rather than as exercises in philosophical allusion. In Florence it was different. That city, proud of its literature, its poets, its philosophers and historians, had always fostered traditions of academic and intellectual excellence and among its painters there flourished a prediliction for secular imagery of the most allusive and often exotic kind. Classical mythology itself had, of course, opened up a whole new mine of imagery, unexplored by the Middle Ages. The gods and goddesses of antiquity, with their complex love lives, their bizarre maraudings, became popular subjects, not only as pretexts for painters to display their technical skills in depicting the human body, but as proof of their own learning, or that of the people who had commissioned them. Sometimes patrons invented a subject for the adornment of their palace walls, or called upon the services of a learned man to provide them. Themes from now virtually unknown poets and chroniclers were used extensively. Looking at a work by a Renaissance artist today one is often unaware of the layers of meaning and significance which he and his contemporaries attached to it. Some subjects, such as Signorelli's *Allegory of Fecundity*, Piero della Francesca's *Scenes from an Allegory*, even Giorgione's *Tempest*, will never be finally interpreted and even the seemingly simple theme of Venus, as depicted by Andrea del Bresciano, Albani or Cambiaso need not necessarily mean the same to us as it did to the *literati* of Florence in the sixteenth century. The goddess herself was a familiar enough figure to the Florentines as the main figure in those many carnival pageants which were enacted to keep the population contented. Naldo Naldi, a contemporary poet, described her in this role:

> 'Through Venus the whole world is therefore renewed, and the leaves of the trees begin to sprout; the happy meadows are painted in varying colours, and the earth sparkles with a multitude of flowers. So let us gaily and rejoicingly follow that goddess, mothers and girls, men, boys and old men, so that we lead a sweet life through her influence, and everyone enjoys his days.'[6]

This was the Venus of Botticelli's *Primavera*, but she was also the figure of poetry, the mistress of the garden of love. Sometimes her nudity could be a sign of physical attractiveness, sometimes a symbol of truth – *nuda veritas*.

But even Botticelli's Venus is not as simple as all that. In a masterly essay Sir E.H. Gombrich has unravelled some of the connotations of the *Primavera*. It was commissioned by Lorenzo di Pierfrancesco de' Medici (1463–1503), the second cousin of Lorenzo de' Medici, for his villa at Castello. He was well known as a man of taste and literary connections, whose mentor had been the humanist and poet Marsilio Ficino. In a letter to his pupil Marsilio identified Venus with Humanity, describing her as:

'a nymph of excellent beauty, born of heaven, and more than all others, beloved by God all highest. Her soul and mind are Love and Charity, her eyes Dignity and Magnanimity, her hands Liberality and Magnificence, her feel Comeliness and Modesty. The whole then, is Temperance and Honesty, Charm and Splendour. Oh, what exquisite beauty! How wonderful to behold!'[7]

This was the image which Lorenzo de Pierfrancesco, prompted by Ficino, must have wanted before his eyes to lead him into that curious amalgam of religious and humanistic virtues. Even more interestingly Botticelli based his actual realization of this 'nymph' on passages from Lucius Apuleius' *The Golden Ass*.

'There entered one of outstanding and wonderful beauty, Venus as a maiden, her naked and partially covered body showed her perfect beauty, for nothing but a flimsy silk garment veiled the lovely maiden. A prying wind now lovingly and lasciviously blew it aside so that the flower of her youth was revealed to the sight, now with a wanton breath made it cling to her, the more graphically to outline the voluptuous form of her limbs . . . . Then there was an inrush of young, fair and unwed maidens, who paid homage to their goddess by scattering flowers, both loose and in bunches, moving in a dance of most exquisite movement. Already the melodious flutes began to play, but far sweeter still, Venus began placidly to move, with a slow, hesitant step, gently swaying her body, slightly inclining her head, and with delicate gestures responded to the voluptuous sound of the flutes'.[8]

This could be a literal description of the *Primavera*, and it is obvious that when Lorenzo de Pierfrancesco commissioned it, when Ficino inspired its creation and when Botticelli painted it, they and most of their contemporaries saw a different painting from that which we see today. And this is true of countless other works of the same period.

That the man who commissioned Botticelli was a Medici underlines the role that his family played in Florentine art, one which was to be of the utmost importance in determining the characteristics of that art, no less than in providing the dynamism for the Renaissance itself. Early in the fifteenth century the elder Cosimo de' Medici had established a pattern when he directed the competition which gave Ghiberti the commission to create the bronze doors of the Baptistry and who, at the end of his life, wrote:

'For fifty years I have done nothing else but earn money, and spend money, and it has become clear to me that spending money gives me greater pleasure than earning it'.[9]

His son Cosimo founded the Medici Library, the first public library to exist in Europe since Roman times, and the model on which Pope Sixtus IV planned the Vatican Library in 1477. Moved at one point to Rome, the library returned to Florence in 1524 when Michelangelo built the Cloisters of San Lorenzo to receive it.

The Medici's first home was the Riccardi Palace in the Via Larga, built by Cosimo in the 1430s; Donatello's *David* stood in the courtyard and other works by him adorned the arches. In the chapel were frescoes by Benozzo Gozzoli, and the whole palace was packed with works of art, ranging from Greek and Roman statues through rare treasures from the orient, to paintings by every Florentine artist of note. Nor were their acquisitions confined to the works of Italian artists. The Medici acquired many of those works by Hugo van der Goes, Joos van Cleve, Dürer and Holbein which give the present galleries of the Uffizi and the Pitti their importance as collections of Northern as well as Italian art. This modest house became what was virtually the first museum in Europe. Lorenzo the Magnificent, the most enlightened member of all the family, doubled these collections in his own lifetime, and when his wife died in 1489, he conceived the idea of converting the villa which he had built for her in the suburb of San Marco into an academy for the training of young artists. It was here that he placed his antique statues, larger paintings, cartoons for murals, and other works of art for which he had no room in his palace in the Via Larga. Michelangelo was among his earliest

10. GIORGIONE (*c.*1476/8–1510)
The Tempest
Oil on canvas, 32 × 28½ in (82 × 73 cm)
Gallerie dell' Accademia, Venice

One of the most famous paintings in the world, this work by Giorgione breathes an air of mystery and magic. Nobody has come up with any adequate explanation of its meaning and it might best be thought of as the pictorial equivalent of a movement from Vivaldi's The Seasons. *Following the example of Giovanni Bellini, Giorgione invents an allegory here which probably has no relationship to any prior written text, being an* invenzioni *or free invention.*

pupils. Lorenzo died in 1492 and two years after his death the Medici were banished from Florence, though in the intervening years they continued the splendour of their activities in Rome. In 1539 after their return, the first Grand Duke moved the family treasures to the Palazzo Vecchio and then to the Pitti Palace where most of them can still be found today.

Even though the Medici were the most famous, the most lavish patrons of the fifteenth century, and they enabled Florentine art to flourish splendidly, they were not unique. There were many courts all over Italy which were rich in works of art commissioned by their rulers, which were usually kept in that portion of the palace known as the *guardaroba*, which had spacious galleries designed to display paintings and sculptures. Smaller objects of more personal significance were kept in the *studio* – more a parlour cum office than the present use of the word would imply, or overflowed into the antechamber, to impress visitors. Typical of these courts was that of Federigo da Montefeltro, Duke of Urbino, described by his contemporaries as the *condottiere virtuose* who gained his love of books, philosophy and art from the humanist and educationalist Vittorino Ramboldoni da Feltre. In the 1430s da Feltre had established a school known as the Casa Zoisa or house of joy, in Mantua where the pupils were

11. SANDRO BOTTICELLI (*c.*1445–1510)
Primavera
Panel, 83 × 127½ in (211 × 324 cm)
Uffizi, Florence

Painted for the same location as Venus Rising From the Sea *and deriving from the same literary source, this vernal lyric, with its linear rhythm and jewel-like colours owes something to earlier artists such as Pollaiuolo, but has a quality peculiar to Botticelli. The* Primavera *exemplifies the new Renaissance convention of the* istoria, '*A story*', wrote Filarete, '*will not bear more than nine figures, rather it should have fewer*'. *This remarkable painting can be regarded as a reworking of the Judgement of Paris or at the same time as a pagan version of the* sacra conversazione, *or sacred conversation, which was the subject of so much fifteenth-century religious art.*

11

taught Greek, Latin, philosophy, mathematics and the fine arts.

Mantua, indeed, became a second Florence, largely because of two people, the painter Mantegna and Isabella d'Este. Artists had for some time been collectors on quite an impressive scale. According to Vasari the sculptor Ghiberti left a number of Graeco-Roman statues and Greek vases; Francesco Squarcione, the Paduan artist who was Mantegna's teacher, travelled through Italy and Greece collecting statues and paintings which he made his pupils copy. His fellow citizen, Sodoma, had a collection which included not only antique statues, medals and bas-reliefs, but also, surprisingly, some medieval works. Mantegna himself was summoned to Mantua in 1460 by the Marquis Lodovico Gonzaga II, to glorify his dynasty with a series of paintings in the *Camera degli Sposi* in the palace, which he did in such a way that the events recorded seemed as though they were really happening, and the wall itself had been dissolved into space. The first of an extraordinary series of artists commissioned by the Gonzaga family, which included Giovanni Bellini, Leonardo, Michelangelo, Perugino, Correggio and Francia, Mantegna was given a princely salary of fifty ducats a month and built a house for himself (which still survives) to display his collection of works of art, which was so impressive that Lorenzo de' Medici made a special journey to Mantua to see it, and the Sforza family from Milan tried hard to buy it. Eventually it was absorbed into the collections of the Gonzaga family, most of which were sold in 1627, with some of the items finding their way into the collection of Charles I of England. Mantegna's own *Triumphs* are still at Hampton Court Palace, near London.

Isabella d'Este was the wife of the next ruler of Mantua, Francesco, who commissioned the Hampton Court paintings, and she herself was an extraordinary woman, described by a contemporary as 'making herself into a kind of burning glass for the art, literature and philosophy of Italy'. She had agents everywhere – in Venice, Rome, Florence, Siena – and she constantly importuned them to buy things for her, or to persuade artists to come to Mantua. Her attempts to get Leonardo to work for her, show not only her attitude to art, but her personal determination. In 1501 she wrote to her agent, Francesco Malatesta, in Florence:

> 'If Leonardo, the Florentine painter is now in Florence, we beg you will inform us what kind of life he is leading, that is to say if he has, as we have been told, started on any commission, and if so what it is, and whether it will involve his staying in Florence. I would be glad if you could find out whether he would be prepared to paint a picture for our studio. If he consents, we would leave the subject, and the time to him, but if he declines, you might at least be able to persuade him to paint for us a little picture of the Madonna, as sweet and holy as his own nature. Will you also beg him to send us another drawing of our portrait [This is now in the Louvre.] since our illustrious Lord has given away the one which he left here? For all of this we shall be as grateful to you as to Leonardo.'[10]

A few weeks later she wrote again saying that she had heard that certain antique vases which had belonged to Lorenzo the Magnificent were on sale, and asked Malatesta to obtain a valuation of 'them from some competent person, such as Leonardo the painter, who used to live in Milan, and is a friend of ours'.[11] Leonardo made no known response to these overtures, and three years later she wrote directly to him:

> 'To Master Leonardo da Vinci, the painter. Hearing that you are settled in Florence, we have begun to hope that our cherished desire to obtain a work from your hand may at last be realized. When you were here in Mantua, and drew our portrait in carbon, you promised us that some day you would paint it in colours. But, because this would be impossible, since you are unable to come to Mantua, we beg you to keep your promise by converting our portrait into another figure, which would be still more acceptable to us; that is to say, a youthful Christ about twelve years, which would be the age He had when He disputed with the doctors in the Temple, executed with all that sweetness and charm of atmosphere which is the peculiar excellence of your art. If you will consent to gratify this, our great desire, remember that, apart from the payment, which you can fix yourself, we shall remain so deeply obliged to you that our sole

desire will be to do what you wish, and from this time forward we are ready to do your service and pleasure, hoping to receive an answer in the affirmative'.[12]

Apart from the ludicrous notion of Leonardo altering a charcoal drawing of a middle-aged Mantuan princess of Neopolitan origin into a painting of a twelve-year-old Christ, there is also evidence of Isabella's surprising tenacity in wishing to secure a work of art; this is typical of the zest of Italian collectors of the time, and also shows the esteem in which the painter's profession was now held.

In Urbino, Guidobaldo II, the son of Federigo, had carried on the enlightened tradition of patronage of the arts started by his father. Castiglione in *The Book of the Courtier* spoke of the Ducal Palace as:

'The most beautiful in Italy, so amply did the Duke provide it with every convenience that it appeared rather a palatial city than a palace. He furnished it not only with the usual wealth of rich brocades, in silk and gold, silver plate and such like, but ornamented it with a vast quantity of ancient statues and bronze sculptures, of fine and rare pictures, and musical instruments of every variety, excluding all but the choicest of objects'.[13]

Encouraged by his wife, the famous and charming Elisabetta, Guidobaldo made the court at Urbino into an arcadia where Raphael met Piero della Francesca and his pupil Melozzo da Forlì, where Signorelli painted some of his most vigorous works, and Cardinal Pietro Bembi, poet, connoisseur and lover of Lucrezia Borgia, walked in the gardens discussing art with Castiglione and Giuliano de' Medici, Duke of Nemours.

The painters of the Montefeltro court often looked towards another centre of painting, Umbria, which had developed a style distinct from that of Florence or Venice, or even Rome. Marked by a certain softness, by the use of broad, compositional conceptions and by soft, evocative lighting, it found its greatest exponents in Perugino, whose sweetness of style was criticized even in his own lifetime, but whose compositions could reach that sense of grandeur which constitutes the main element of his legacy to his pupil Raphael, and by Pinturicchio, whose main patrons were Pope Pius II, and Alexander VI. This eminently marketable style, deprecated though it has been by the more austere tastes of the first half of the twentieth century, had a wide influence. It can be seen for instance in the works of Andrea del Sarto (1486–1531), which combine Florentine classicism with an almost melancholic lyricism, with over-emphasized lighting effects and an over-conscious emphasis on the tactile quality of surfaces. At the same time, however, del Sarto refined still further the subtleties of portraiture, his excellence in this area being passed on to his pupil Pontormo.

Even though the patronage of the Medici family was magnificent, and that of other dynasties such as the Sforza in Milan, the Gonzagas in Mantua, the Montefeltro family in Urbino was extensive, they palled into near insignificance when compared with the patronage being exercized by the papacy. There were many reasons for this. Unlike secular dynasties, subject to political vicissitudes and dynastic accidents, the papacy, since the healing of the Avignon schism, had a built-in continuity. Moreover, it possessed a powerful ideological reason for the expenditure of vast sums on works of art. Dedicated to the Glory of God and the edification of the faithful, the papacy also emphasized the spiritual, and the political pre-eminence of the bishops of Rome, who saw themselves as the terrestrial vice-regents of the Almighty. This process of functional glorification became all the more important as the very basis of papal power came under attack from Protestantism. Never before had conspicuous expenditure been so important for both doctrinal and political reasons.

12

12. PIERO DELLA FRANCESCA
(c.1410/20–92)
Federigo da Montefeltro, Duke of Urbino
Panel, $18\frac{1}{2} \times 12\frac{1}{2}$ in (47 × 32 cm)
Uffizi, Florence

One of the great portraits of the Renaissance, the psychological realism and striking quality of this picture of a man who was both a brilliant politician and an enlightened patron of the arts, owes much of its effectiveness to the dramatic siting of the head and the unexpected simplicity of the colour. Federigo was Piero's most important patron and much of his work was produced for the Duke's Palace in Urbino. The portrait was praised in a poem of 1466.

13

14

VINCENTII DESIDERII VITVM
FRANCIE EXPRESSVM MANV

15

97

13. PAOLO UCCELLO (c.1396/7–1475)
The Battle of San Romano
Panel, 125½ × 70 in (320 × 179 cm)
Uffizi, Florence

This picture was painted twenty years after the event for Cosimo de' Medici the Elder, to commemorate the battle which the Florentines won over the Milanese on 1 June 1432. The panel shown here is one of three, the others being in the National Gallery, London and the Louvre. The arbitrary colouring, the dazzlingly brilliant effects of perspective and the simplification of the forms are suggestive of those qualities in Uccello's work which endeared him to so many artists of the twentieth century, such as Leger and Dali. In the San Romano panels Uccello would seem to be more concerned with sustaining the illusion of a grand commemorative pageant to the glories of courtly aristocratic warfare, than with recording the actualities of war. The newly invented rules of perspective are used experimentally, for their own sake, rather than applied specifically to the battle scene.

14. GENTILE DA FABRIANO
(c.1370–1427)
Adoration of the Magi
Panel, 117½ × 108¼ in (299 × 276 cm)
Uffizi, Florence

There is still something of the magic of the Medieval spirit in this sumptuous altarpiece painted for the church of S. Trinita in Florence, where it remained until the nineteenth century. The wealth of detail is reminiscent of a Burgundian illuminated book of hours, but the perspective skills are of the Renaissance. Gentile, an Umbrian who had been court painter for the Doge's Palace at Venice, introduced a strongly romantic element to the more austere conventions of contemporary Florentine art. The use of exotic animals and a traditional gilded sky signify his relation both to the immediate Medieval past and to the decorative interests which remained popular with Florentine patrons.

15. FRANCESCO RAIBOLINI known as
FRANCESCO FRANCIA (c.1450–1517/18)
St. Stephen
Panel, 29½ × 20¾ in (75 × 53 cm)
Galleria Borghese, Rome

Facing the stones which killed him, trickles of blood pouring down his head, St. Stephen as portrayed by Francia seems to belong to an earlier period than the artist. He was painted in 1475, as a votive offering commissioned by one Vincenzo Desiderio, whose name is linked with that of the artist on the lable painted on lower left. Following the traditions of Alberti's aesthetics, Francia's aim is to be lifelike rather than to establish a psychological identity for the young saint, who is arbitrarily placed before a conventional Umbrian landscape which owes much to Perugino.

16. PIERO DELLA FRANCESCA
(1410/20–92)
Battista Sforza
Panel, 18½ × 12½ in (47 × 32 cm)
Uffizi, Florence

Painted in Urbino in the late 1460s, this portrait is of the Milanese wife of the Duke of Urbino and shows the subject looking much older than twenty, her age at this time. The fine precision of her jewellery is matched by the luminous detail of the landscape. Piero's portrait of Battista, who died in 1472, was almost certainly painted as a companion piece to his earlier portrait of her husband Federigo, probably from a death mask. The form of the profile portrait was often so powerful that the individuality of the sitter was greatly sacrificed to it.

17. PIERO DELLA FRANCESCA
Scene from an Allegory
Panel, 18½ × 12½ in (47 × 32 cm)
Uffizi, Florence

In front of the Duchess are the Theological Virtues, and two saints stand behind her. Piero has added to the typical Renaissance idea of the Triumph an intense poetic feeling, and a ravishing stillness. Drawn along by mythical beasts, the Duchess presides over an allegory in which Piero has combined the beauties of the Umbrian landscape with the iconography of classical Antiquity and Italy's Christian heritage. Here, the aim of the artist was to stress the political continuity and cultural stability achieved under her husband's rule.

16

17

18

18. GENTILE BELLINI (*c.*1429–1507)
The Miracle of the Relic of the True Cross
Oil on canvas, 127 × 169 in (323 × 430 cm)
Gallerie dell' Accademia, Venice

Bellini has chosen the canal of S. Lorenzo to depict an incident when the reliquary dropped into the water, but did not sink. This painting was commissioned by the Scuola (or Guild) of St. John the Evangelist, whose members are seen on the right. These Guilds were important patrons of art, *especially in Venice. Gentile applies the conventions of fixed point perspective to create a sense of reality. At the same time he shows little apparent interest in coping with the considerably difficult problem of how to present a crowd scene convincingly.*

19. GIOVANNI BELLINI (*c.*1430–1516)
Fickle Fortune
Panel, $13\frac{1}{4} \times 8\frac{1}{2}$ in (34 × 22 cm)
Gallerie dell' Accademia, Venice

Replete with complex symbols typical of the fifteenth and sixteenth centuries, the precise meaning of this work is now obscure, however obvious its basic significance may be. However, the luminous evening sky, the landscape with its folded hills and the mysterious presence of Fortune herself *all seem to transcend the centuries. As in A Sacred Allegory, Bellini combines a strongly classical range of imagery with an essentially modern landscape. He thus emphasizes the continuity of cultural values, whilst bringing their representation up-to-date.*

20

20. GIOVANNI BELLINI
The Madonna with John the Baptist and another
Saint
Panel, 21 × 30 in (54 × 76 cm)
Gallerie dell' Accademia, Venice

Perhaps more than any other of Giovanni Bellini's paintings, this statuesque yet gentle composition with its mixed landscape background shows the debt which later Venetians owed to his mastery of light and colour. Unlike earlier Renaissance painters, Bellini constructs his figures as *sculptural forms which contrasted with the exquisite 'humanist' landscape behind them. The religious significance of the scene is thus made to seem a part of everyday life, while at the same time being an idealized version of it in fashionable Neo-Platonic terms.*

21

21. ANDREA DA MURANO
(*c.*1430–1502)
Triptych
Panel: central section $59\frac{3}{4} \times 34\frac{1}{2}$ in (152×88 cm),
sides $59\frac{3}{4} \times 18\frac{1}{2}$ in (152×47 cm), lunette $31\frac{1}{2} \times 78\frac{1}{4}$ in
(80×199 cm)
Gallerie dell' Accademia, Venice

A work of his youth, this triptych shows Andrea da Murano at his most engaging. Despite the sophistication of parts of the painting, he still adheres to Medieval concepts of relative size. Ecclesiastical patrons often demanded the retention of such anti-naturalistic features as the gilded ground behind the saints. Indeed, the very form of the triptych encourages a more decorative approach to the arrangement of the human body, which has to fill in the rectangular space allotted it.

22

22. ANTONELLO DA MESSINA
(c.1430–79)
Portrait of an Unknown Man
Panel, $13\frac{1}{4} \times 9\frac{1}{4}$ in (34×24 cm)
Galleria Borghese, Rome

The constructional skill with which Antonello has modelled this face seems to look forward to the art of the twentieth century. At the same time his powers of perception are displayed in the look of quizzical good humour in the sitter's eyes, and the smile hovering on his lips. Antonello was one of the earliest fifteenth-century Italian painters to master the Flemish technique of painting in oils. The resulting realism of detail guaranteed him a steady stream of patrons, eager to be portrayed more convincingly than ever before in portraiture.

23. ANDREA MANTEGNA (c.1431–1506)
Cardinal Carlo de' Medici
Panel, $16 \times 11\frac{3}{4}$ in (41×30 cm)
Uffizi, Florence

Once thought to be a portrait of Ludovico Gonzaga, the Protonotary Apostolic at Mantua, this is now generally taken as being of Cardinal Carlo de' Medici, the illegitimate son of Cosimo the Elder, and a slave – hence his swarthy complexion. Mantegna's portrait seems to have been influenced by deliberate Flemish disregard for the profile conventions of earlier Italian portraiture whilst remaining strongly sculptural in its overall effect.

23

24

24. ANDREA MANTEGNA
St. George
Panel, 26 × 12½ in (66 × 32 cm)
Gallerie dell' Accademia, Venice

This is one of the most delightful paintings of the fifteenth century, despite the rather dish-like quality of the saint's halo. The decorative swag which hangs between the two framing columns at once introduces us to the world of classical architecture and of natural abundance. Mantegna's deeply romantic vision of Antiquity is ideally set off here by the simple landscape, in which the winding road is playfully made to take the traditional role of the dragon.

25. DOMENICO VENEZIANO (c.1435–61)
Madonna with Saints
Panel, 82 × 83¾ in (209 × 213 cm)
Gallerie dell' Accademia, Venice

The pale delicacy of the Florentine tradition superimposed upon the romantic effulgence which he had acquired from his native Venice, gives the work of Domenico a unique place in the mixed traditions of Italian art. Borrowing his male saints from Donatello, Veneziano creates the perfect analogue of Albertian space, at the same time moulding a form from a regular light source in a manner which profoundly influenced his two major pupils, Andrea del Castagno and Piero della Francesca. Veneziano's small oeuvre constitutes the most exquisite blend of international Gothic and early Renaissance sensibility in all fifteenth-century Italian art.

26

26. FRANCESCO DEL COSSA
(1435–77)
Extinguishing a Fire
Panel, $11\frac{3}{4} \times 84\frac{1}{2}$ in (30×215 cm)
Musei Vaticani, Rome

This record of one of the miracles of S. Vincenzo Ferreri is one of the two panels of a triptych. The centre piece is in the National Gallery, London, the other wing in the art gallery at Brera. Apart from its meticulous observance of contemporary reality, the painting exudes an atmosphere akin to that achieved by some surrealists of the twentieth century. The picture exemplifies the Albertian ideal of vivacitas or liveliness, fusing together the influences of Botticelli and Leonardo da Vinci in a strikingly unusual manner. Cossa's best known works are frescoes in the Palazzo di Schifanoia.

27. ANDREA DEL VERROCCHIO
(c.1435–88)
The Baptism of Christ
Panel, $69\frac{1}{2} \times 59\frac{1}{4}$ in (177×151 cm)
Uffizi, Florence

Painted about 1475 for the church of S. Salvi, this painting did not enter the Uffizi till 1919. It is generally accepted that the angel on the left was painted by Leonardo, but not, as was once believed, the landscape background. Leonardo was apprenticed to Verrocchio at the age of 17 and he was fortunate to be trained in a workshop which was already familiar with the realism of Flemish landscape painting. Leonardo's angel stands out markedly against the more three-dimensional style of the central figures, which remind us that Verrocchio was also famous as a sculptor.

28. QUIRIZIO DA MURANO (c.1440–72)
Christ and a Nun
Panel, $44\frac{3}{4} \times 34$ in (114×87 cm)
Gallerie dell' Accademia, Venice

The influence of both Crivelli and Bellini is to be seen in this work by yet another distinguished artist from the small island of Murano outside Venice. Traditionalism and inventiveness go hand in hand in this serene work. Late fifteenth-century Venetian painting tended to be highly traditional. The dominant tendency, as represented here, was to selectively attach some aspects of Florentine naturalism to a traditional sense of formal design.

27

28

29

30

29. PIERO DEL POLLAIUOLO (c.1441-96)
St. Jerome
Panel, 18 × 10 in (46 × 26 cm)
Pitti, Florence

Although at times attributed to Piero di Cosimo and other artists, the original ascription of this work to Pollaiuolo given to it by Cardinal Leopoldo de' Medici seems to be the right one. More than any other painter, Pollaiuolo carried forward Masaccio's passion for the volumetric qualities of Roman art, together with an overriding naturalism. This head of Jerome is unimaginable without the example of late Roman portrait sculpture. At the same time it is clearly and recognizably taken from life. It was the energy with which Pollaiuolo revitalized the Antique which gained him his wide reputation. Traditionally Piero's work was felt to be inferior to that of his brother Antonio.

30. SANDRO BOTTICELLI (c.1445-1510)
Calumny
Panel, 24½ × 35¾ in (62 × 9 cm)
Uffizi, Florence

This painting embodying a typical Renaissance concept was designed to recreate a lost painting by the famous Greek artist Apelles, and was commissioned from Botticelli by Antonio Segni, a scholarly friend of Leonardo da Vinci. It dates from the last decade of the fifteenth century when the artist was going through a religious crisis. In his celebrated Treatise on Painting *Alberti had particularly recom-* mended to young artists Lucian's story of the Calumny of Apelles as a morally uplifting theme from which to construct an istoria or history painting of which Botticelli quickly became the master interpreter. The Calumny is in effect a perfect example of how Alberti's young contemporaries looked to his treatise as a text-book as well as a good example of Botticelli's subtle feeling for contour.

31. SANDRO BOTTICELLI
Judith
Panel, 85 × 56 in (31 × 24 cm)
Uffizi, Florence

This is a dramatic evocation of a theme which was very popular with Florentine artists of the fifteenth century because of its implied vindication of national liberty. It was part of a diptych, the other panel representing Judith in the tent of Holofernes. The panels were commissioned by Rodolfo Sirigatti, who presented them to Francesco de' Medici. The vivid dynamism of the linear pattern suggests movement and excitement.

33

32. SANDRO BOTTICELLI
Venus Rising from the Sea
Oil on canvas, $67 \times 108\frac{1}{2}$ in (171×277 cm)
Uffizi, Florence

Probably one of the most famous paintings in the world, Botticelli's serene classical vision of a Graeco-Roman myth was commissioned by Lorenzo di Pierfrancesco de' Medici for his country house at Castello near Florence. The artist had just returned from Rome where he had been working on the Sistine Chapel, and the literary source was a poem by Angelo Poliziano, the favourite poet of the Medici family at

that time. The philosopher Ficino wrote to Lorenzo, 'Your Luna – the continuous motion of your soul and body . . . should fix her eyes on Venus herself, that is to say on humanity. For humanity herself is a nymph of excellent comeliness and modesty, born of heaven and more than others beloved by God all highest.' How extraordinary and heretical this would have seemed a century previously!

33. PERUGINO (*c.*1445/50–1523)
Portrait of Francesco delle Opere
Panel, $20 \times 16\frac{3}{4}$ in (51×43 cm)
Uffizi, Florence

The airy landscape in the background adds a new dimension to the Flemish-like realism of this portrait of a man holding in his hands the inscription 'Timete Deum' or 'Fear God'.

Such highly naturalistic portraiture very quickly super- seded the older more decorative tradition of Piero della Francesca, who had at one time been Perugino's teacher.

34. PERUGINO
Mary Magdalen
Panel, $18\frac{1}{2} \times 13\frac{1}{4}$ in (47×34 cm)
Pitti, Florence

Although clearly a portrait, the name 'S. Maria Mag- dalena' on the top of the model's dress indicates the subject. The work reflects the influence of Verrocchio and is

suggestive of the style of Raphael. Perugino specialized in a particular kind of ideal beauty and was an important teacher, his most celebrated pupil being Raphael.

34

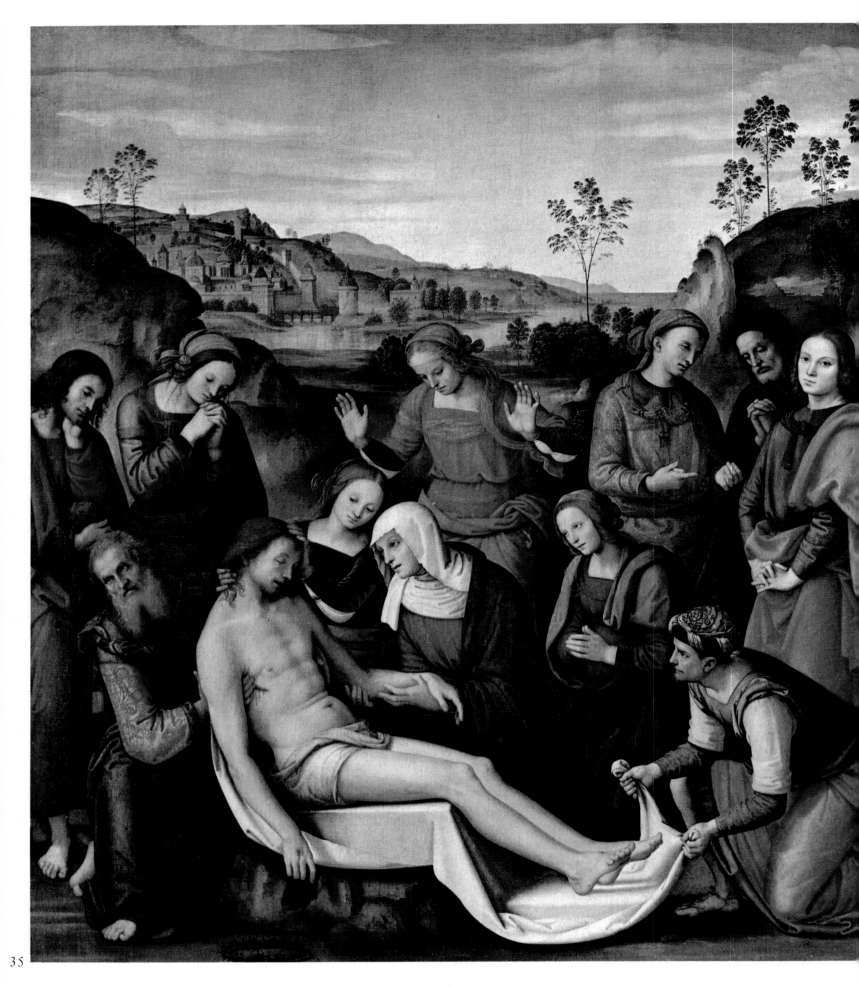

35

35. PERUGINO
The Deposition
Panel, $84\frac{1}{4} \times 76\frac{1}{2}$ in (214×195 cm)
Pitti, Florence

This ambitious composition, in which the painter attempts to give meaning and compositional significance to twelve different figures, indicates the new level of artistic sophistication which Italian painting was beginning to achieve in the opening years of the fifteenth century. It was painted for *the nuns of S. Chiara in Florence. In many ways Perugino's later work anticipates the heavily stylized rhetoric of the High Renaissance, whilst retaining an abundance of detail which is sometimes at odds with the monumentality of his overall pictorial intentions.*

36

37

36. BARTOLOMMEO MONTAGNA
(1450–1523)
The Madonna with St. Jerome and St. Sebastian
Panel, 85 × 63½ in (216 × 162 cm)
Gallerie dell' Accademia, Venice

Montagna here provides us with a good example of a provincial painter learning to come to terms with the latest fashions in Tuscan art in the latter half of the fifteenth century. The result is a somewhat uncomfortable fusion of Venetian colour painting with a far more linear tradition. Montagna's work was influenced by Giovanni Bellini.

37. LEONARDO DA VINCI (1452–1519)
The Annunciation
Panel, 38½ × 85¼ in (98 × 217 cm)
Uffizi, Florence

A youthful work done probably when Leonardo was in Verrocchio's workshop, the authenticity of this work, with its loving depiction of nature, is proven by the existence of a preliminary drawing related to it. The blending of the landscape into the sky is especially Leonardoesque. This is one of Leonardo's sweetest pictures and shows him beginning to experiment with the technique of sfumato, or modelling from light to dark, which became an increasing preoccupation. The little altar is a typical piece of Leonardo's wit and archaeological observation.

38. LEONARDO DA VINCI
St. Jerome
Oil on canvas, 40½ × 29½ in (103 × 75 cm)
Musei Vaticani, Rome

This unusual image of the saint in the desert, which Leonardo commenced in Florence in 1482, was left unfinished when he moved to Milan. The anatomical certainties of the figure are especially noticeable. The St. Jerome is characteristic of Leonardo's hostility to the direct imitation of classical models, and at the same time stands in a long line of images of old age, which are frequently contrasted to images of youth. His last words in 1519 were, 'While I thought that I was learning to live, I have been learning how to die.'

38

41

39. LEONARDO DA VINCI
The Adoration of The Magi
Detail of a panel, $95\frac{1}{2} \times 96\frac{3}{4}$ in (243×246 cm)
Uffizi, Florence

It is only in the close examination of a large sketch such as that for The Adoration of the Magi *that it is possible completely to appreciate the spontaneous mastery of line which made Leonardo one of the greatest draughtsmen of all time. In this large blocked-in sketch Leonardo broke decisively with the Albertian conventions of the* istoria *in the interests of psychological innovation. The Adoration is*

all but swamped by the tumultuous crowd which gathers round, and by the extraordinary scenes behind of men and horses rushing forward. Vasari noted that it was, 'the instability of his character' which 'caused him to take up and abandon many things'. We might rather say that it was the stability of his nature which allowed him to attempt so much in so short a time.

40. BERNADINO PINTURICCHIO
(c.1454–1513)
The Crucifixion
Panel, $22\frac{1}{2} \times 15\frac{3}{4}$ in (57×40 cm)
Galleria Borghese, Rome

The delicate splendour of Pinturicchio's vision of the Crucifixion *turns it almost into a joyous event. The figures of St. Christopher and St. Jerome, which create a marvellous compositional counterpoint, contrast with the*

river which winds into the landscape to create an immense feeling of depth. A contemporary of Perugino and a fellow Umbrian, Pinturicchio's work is often all but overwhelmed by his love of very clear, bright colours.

41. VITTORE CARPACCIO
(c.1460/5–1523/6)
The English Ambassadors at the Breton Court
Oil on canvas, $108 \times 231\frac{3}{4}$ in (275×589 cm)
Gallerie dell' Accademia, Venice

Commissioned for the Guild of St. Ursula in 1489, these paintings were hung originally in the chapel of the Guild near the church of S. Giovannie Paolo. After the Guild was suppressed by Napoleon in 1810, the pictures passed to the Accademia. There are nine episodes of the history. This

scene, from a cycle illustrating the life and martyrdom of St. Ursula, creates a characteristically Venetian vision of splendour and opulence from the raw material of Florentine and north Italian art. The ideal architecture is a perfect foil for this most imaginative of documentary painters.

42. VITTORE CARPACCIO
The Miracle of the Reliquary of the True Cross
Oil on canvas, $155\frac{1}{2} \times 153$ in (395×389 cm)
Gallerie dell' Accademia, Venice

This is the first realistic view we know of the Grand Canal in Venice, with the old, wooden bridge of the Rialto, later to be replaced by the present stone structure. Quite apart from the breathtaking accuracy of the view which Carpaccio presents, there is the poetic beauty of the sky so lovingly depicted in its evening splendour. Carpaccio has here resolved the problem of crowd scenes which Gentile Bellini had felt able to ignore in his painting of the same subject. Carpaccio plays here with the typically Venetian chimney stacks just as elsewhere he plays with hats and carpets in the following two pictures. We should again note the little dog in the gondola at the bottom right of the picture.

43

44

45

43. VITTORE CARPACCIO
St. Ursula and the Prince Taking Leave
Oil on canvas (slightly cut at top and sides)
110 × 240½ in (280 × 611 cm)
Gallerie dell' Accademia, Venice

The picture is divided by the flagpole into two scenes. On the left the English prince is shown saying his farewell to his father; on the right the engaged couple are taking leave of the girl's parents. The figures may be members of the Loredan family, who were patrons of the Guild. We should note the Turkish and oriental rugs which are so much a part of Carpaccio's world, rooted as it is in the accumulated wealth of the Venetian trading empire.

44. VITTORE CARPACCIO
The Meeting with the Pope
Oil on canvas, 110¼ × 120¾ in (281 × 307 cm)
Gallerie dell' Accademia, Venice

The conglomeration of cardinals and standard bearers in the middle of the picture adds a sense of activity to a scene which has a strangely dramatic quality about it. Carpaccio clearly enjoyed creating the effect of the cardinals' hats which enjoy a life of their own within the picture, and give a visual focus to the tragic events of the story of St. Ursula.

45. VITTORE CARPACCIO
The Dream of St. Ursula
Detail of an oil on canvas, 126½ × 117¼ in (274 × 267 cm)
Gallerie dell' Accademia, Venice

The Flemish qualities which had begun to exert an influence on Venetian art some decades earlier are very apparent in the meticulously evenly-lit interior of this room – a document of interest to the social historian no less than to the critic. Carpaccio's love of abstract patterning is clearly apparent in the immensely strong overall design of this scene, in which the angel advances in a steady beam of light to the foot of the bed in which Ursula lies asleep. The little dog at the foot of the bed is almost a hall-mark of Carpaccio's work and regularly appears elsewhere.

46

HOC OPVS SVMPTIBVS DOMNI ANTHONII DE CHARITATE CA
NONICI ECCLESIE DE CONVERSANÓ IN FORMA M R E D ACTVM EST 147·

47

48

46. ALVISE VIVARINI (*fl.*1457–*c*1503–5)
St. John the Baptist
Panel, 68¾ × 77 in (175 × 196 cm)
Gallerie dell' Accademia, Venice

The graceful elegance of the saint's figure is emphasized by the long, pointing finger, the flowing lines of the green cloak contrasting with those of the white undergarment. There is a rare delicacy in the modelling of the face, and the emphasis on the muscles and tendons of the body. Vivarini worked in and around Venice in the mid-fifteenth century, and adapted the extreme three-dimensionality of so much contemporary Florentine art to the local idiom.

47. BARTOLOMMEO VIVARINI
(*fl.*1450–99)
The Nativity
Panel, 51½ × 19 in (131 × 49 cm)
Gallerie dell' Accademia, Venice

Painted, according to the inscription, in 1475 for the church of Conversano, this moving version of the birth of Christ has an air of Gothic intensity and is far removed from the humanistic sophistication of works by contemporaries such as Piero della Francesca or Botticelli. In this central panel from an altarpiece which would originally have consisted of many separate images, Vivarini was happy to combine the apparition of the angel to the shepherds with a Nativity scene in a manner which looks back to earlier Medieval art. Bartolommeo worked in partnership with his brother.

48. LUCA SIGNORELLI (*c.*1441–1523)
Allegory of Fecundity
Oil on canvas, 24 × 42¾ in (61 × 109 cm)
Uffizi, Florence

Another of those elaborately charged symbolic scenes which so delighted the minds of the Renaissance, this monochromatic painting by Signorelli suggests the influence of classical bas-reliefs and emphasizes his concern with a certain wiry, anatomical realism. Signorelli's heroic nudes pursue one aspect of Piero della Francesca's work – the emphasis on highly statuesque tonal modelling which becomes almost an end in itself.

49. FILIPPINO LIPPI (c.1458–1504)
The Adoration of the Magi
Panel, 101 × 94½ in (257 × 241 cm)
Uffizi, Florence

Inscribed on the back with the artist's name and the date, 29 March, 1496, this picture was painted for the church of San Donato near Florence to take the place of one left unfinished by Leonardo – whose influence it shows, especially in the pyramidal composition. The young Magi being crowned is Giovanni di Pierfrancesco, who became the father of the famous condottiere *Giovanni delle Bande Nere. The* central figure of the Virgin and Child, together with the twisting contraposto *kneeling worshipper, were almost undoubtedly drawn from Leonardo's work, although the overall style owes far more to Botticelli's many versions of this same subject. The ground is strewn with fragments of classical architecture which, as so often in the painting of this period, suggests its destined cultural milieu.*

50. PIERO DI COSIMO (1462–1521)
The Immaculate Conception
Panel, $81 \times 67\frac{1}{2}$ in (206×172 cm)
Uffizi, Florence

Combining in a curiously attractive way the traditions of the fifteenth century with the new currents of the sixteenth, Piero's works have a compelling magic of their own.

Despite the fact that this painting has been heavily retouched, we can still sense that fantastical quality in the figures and details of the surrounding landscape.

51

51. FRA BARTOLOMEO DELLA
PORTA (1475–1515)
The Adoration of the Child Jesus
Panel, 43¾ in (112 cm) in diameter
Galleria Borghese, Rome

This, the oldest painting in the Borghese Gallery, is a youthful work of the artist and shows the influence of Piero di Cosimo, and above all of Raphael, from whose formal innovations – the rounded form itself and the relation of Virgin to Child – so much of Fra Bartolomeo's work ultimately derives.

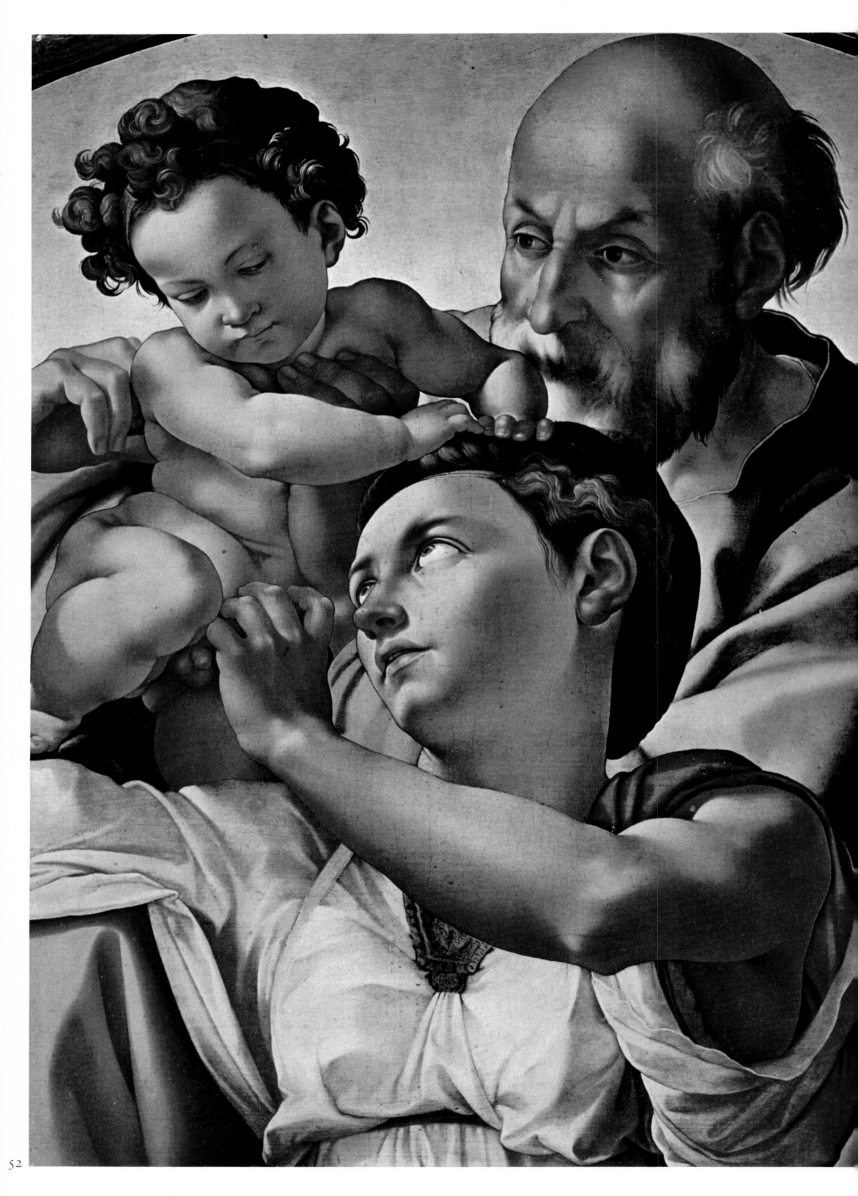

52. MICHELANGELO BUONARROTI
(1475–1564)
The Holy Family
Detail of a panel, 47 in (120 cm) in diameter
Uffizi, Florence

The amazing structural solidity of the painting comes close to the three-dimensional appearance of sculpture, an effect which is heightened by the skilful use of colour. This is possibly part of the altarpiece on which it is recorded that

Michelangelo was working in Rome in 1500. The idealized figures of the Holy Family also bear witness to Michelangelo's dislike of naturalism especially as evinced in Flemish painting.

53. MICHELANGELO BUONARROTI
The Flood
Detail of a fresco cycle occupying an area of
approximately 5597 sq ft (520 m²)

Ceiling of the Sistine Chapel, Rome

Michelangelo's mastery of the human form and his ability to coalesce a variety of movements and situations into a convincing unity, are revealed in this segment of the ceiling. Alberti had established the human figure as the focal point of fifteenth-century aesthetics. It was Michelangelo, some

fifty years later, who gave that aesthetic its most heroic form. 'Good painting,' he wrote, 'is nothing but a copy of the perfection of God and a recollection of this in painting; it is a music and a melody which only intellect can understand, and that with great difficulty.'

135

54

54. GIORGIONE (1477–1510)
The Three Ages of Man
Panel, $24\frac{1}{2} \times 30\frac{1}{4}$ in (62×77 cm)
Pitti, Florence

This work has been variously attributed to Lorenzo Lotto and Giovanni Bellini, but despite its bad state of preservation, which makes accurate attribution difficult, it is now generally conceded to be by Giorgione. Although The Three Ages of Man *was a popular theme at the time, it is* doubtful whether this is an appropriate title. Giorgione's technical debt to Leonardo can clearly be appreciated here, in the soft sfumato *modelling and in the entire construction of the picture space, from light to dark which gives a sense of mystery and drama.*

55. GIORGIONE
The Trial of Moses
Panel, $35 \times 28\frac{1}{4}$ in (89×72 cm)
Uffizi, Florence

Originally ascribed to Giovanni Bellini, this is now accepted as a work of Giorgione, although it has been finished by another hand. The story is that of Moses who, when an infant, took the crown from Pharaoh's head, and put it on his own and had to submit to trial by ordeal; in choosing fire he proved his innocence. Giorgione was extremely famous in his own lifetime, and when Isabella d'Este wanted one of his pictures for her collection she simply asked for 'a Giorgione' rather than attempting to commission a specific image.

55

56

56. GIOVANNI GEROLAMO
SAVOLDO (1480–*c*1548)
Tobias and the Angel
Panel, $37\frac{1}{2} \times 49\frac{1}{2}$ in (96 × 126 cm)
Galleria Borghese, Rome

Born in Brescia, but working in Venice, Salvoldo exemplifies in his glowing colours, dramatic composition and evocative landscape, the basic tradition of the great Venetians. Salvoldo combines the chiaroscuro effect which Leonardo's followers had made fashionable throughout northern Italy, with the colour tonality of Giorgione.

57. PALMA IL VECCHIO (1480–c1528)
Sacred Conversation Piece
Oil on canvas, 50 × 76½ in (127 × 195 cm)
Gallerie dell' Accademia, Venice

Originally experiencing the influence of Carpaccio and then of Giorgione, by the time he painted this picture Palma was reflecting the looser handling and brighter colours of Titian. *The Madonna here is derived from Titian's celebrated* Pesaro Madonna *in the Frari church in Venice which showed Titian's fully developed personal style.*

58. RAFFAELLO SANZIO called
RAPHAEL (1483–1520)
Agnolo Doni
Panel, 24¾ × 17¾ in (63 × 45 cm)
Pitti, Florence

'Averse to spending money for other things, but for paintings or sculpture, in which he greatly delighted he would willingly pay', Agnolo Doni commissioned these portraits of himself and his wife in the opening years of the sixteenth century. They were bought for the Pitti by Grand Duke Leopold II in about 1815. *Raphael's portrait is clearly influenced by the model provided by his teacher, Perugino. The three-quarter profile was particularly favoured by Raphael in his portraiture and demonstrates his great powers of draughtsmanship.*

58

60

59. RAPHAEL
The Madonna del Granduca
Panel, $33\frac{1}{4} \times 21\frac{1}{2}$ in (85×55 cm)
Pitti, Florence

Known as The Madonna of the Grand Duke *this work owes its name to the Grand Duke Ferdinando III, who bought it in 1799 and was passionately attached to it. It represents the apogee of Raphael's Florentine manner. Profoundly influenced by Leonardo, Raphael uses his* chiaroscuro *effects to much less dramatic ends in order to underline the relationship of Mother to Child. There is none of that complexity which is common to Leonardo's similar scenes. Raphael is content to achieve a much simpler overall impact.*

60. RAPHAEL
The Madonna of the Chair
Oil on canvas, $27\frac{3}{4}$ in (71 cm) in diameter
Pitti, Florence

Probably the most famous of Raphael's many Madonnas, this was painted in 1516 at the time when the artist was working on the Vatican Stanze. Its clarity and purity of line suggest the influence that classical Rome had exercised on *him. It was in this style of painting that Raphael abstracted the essence of Michelangelo's extraordinary but sometimes bizarre idealism into a supremely confident and monumental idiom of his own.*

61. RIDOLFO DEL GHIRLANDAIO
(1483–1561)
The Goldsmith
Panel, $16\frac{3}{4} \times 12$ in (43×31 cm)
Pitti, Florence

The title, though of long standing, stems merely from the fact that the subject is examining a piece of jewellery. It was bought for Cardinal Leopoldo de' Medici as a Leonardo and attributed to Ghirlandaio in the nineteenth century.

Whoever actually painted this portrait, we can detect the influence of Domenico Ghirlandaio, especially in the highly idiosyncratic painting of the eyes. Ridolfo was Domenico Ghirlandaio's son and a close friend of Raphael.

62. RIDOLFO DEL GHIRLANDAIO
Portrait of a Woman
Panel, $24 \times 18\frac{1}{2}$ in (61×47 cm)
Pitti, Florence

Dated 1509, this Raphaelesque portrait is marked by its fine draughtsmanship, cool, even light and soberly emphatic colouring. The early fifteenth-century practice of placing a sitter against a plain monochrome background survived well into the sixteenth century, giving the sitter an emblematic appearance derived from Roman portrait medallions.

63

64

63. ANDREA DEL SARTO (1486–1530)
The Assumption
Panel, 149 × 87¼ in (379 × 222 cm)
Pitti, Florence

Andrea del Sarto painted two versions of this – both of them in the Pitti. This particular picture was painted in 1526 for the chapel of the Passerini family in Cortona. At this point we can recognize all the most characteristic elements of High Renaissance art – its idealized classical forms and its highly inventive arrangement of large numbers of figures in a very shallow picture space. Andrea's frescoes in SS. Annunziata also epitomize the High Renaissance style.

64. ANDREA DEL SARTO
The Story of Joseph
Panel, 38½ × 53 in (93 × 135 cm)
Pitti, Florence

Here the artist has grouped together within one painting all the principal events in Joseph's life, distributing them throughout the composition with rare skill. The extraordinary angle of the staircase, and the almost distracted relationship between different areas of the composition should already probably be classified as Mannerist. There is a close copy of this picture by Pontormo in the National Gallery, London, which is further exaggerated.

65

66

65. ANDREA DEL SARTO
Holy Family
Panel, $55 \times 40\frac{3}{4}$ in (140×104 cm)
Pitti, Florence

Painted for Ottaviano de' Medici c1529 this picture shows the influence of Leonardo in the triangular composition and of Michelangelo in the articulation of the figures. Gone are the sweet landscape backgrounds of Perugino and early Holy Family paintings in favour of a much more abstract and intellectual approach to pictorial composition.

66. ANDREA DEL SARTO
The Story of Joseph
Panel, $38\frac{1}{2} \times 53$ in (98×135 cm)
Pitti, Florence

This was commissioned by Pierfrancesco Borgherini 'for furnishing a room'. It shows an episode in Joseph's life, including his service to Pharaoh. Joseph was an Old Testament hero who won the favour of the Egyptian Pharaoh by interpreting a dream and obtained a high place in that ancient kingdom.

147

67

69

67. GIOVANNI BATTISTA
BENVENUTI called ORTOLANO
(1489–c1527)
The Deposition
Panel, 103¾ × 78 in (264 × 202 cm)
Galleria Borghese, Rome

Painted for a church in Ferrara, this painting shows the wide range of devices which were being evolved at the beginning of the sixteenth century to depict drama and emotion, and *which would be formulated into a grammar of expression. The most important source for this new and highly stylized rhetoric was Raphael's* Deposition.

68. MARCO BASAITI (fl.1493–1530)
Dawn Prayer
Detail of a panel, 145½ × 88 in (371 × 224 cm)
Gallerie dell' Accademia, Venice

Painted in 1516 this detail shows the influence Giorgione had on his contemporaries. The fortified hill-town may be partially imagined, but it undoubtedly resembles what *many small north Italian towns and fortresses must have been like in the early sixteenth century, although the soldiers clearly derive from classical Antiquity.*

69. JACOPO PONTORMO (1494–1557)
Portrait of Cosimo de' Medici the Elder
Panel, 34 × 25½ in (87 × 65 cm)
Uffizi, Florence

A posthumous portrait of Lorenzo de' Medici's grandfather, who had been exiled from Florence in 1433, this image of the old merchant exudes an indefinable sense of *melancholy. Lorenzo had been the greatest Florentine patron of the late fifteenth century, dying in 1492, and he gained the Medici banking privileges from Sixtus IV.*

70. GIOVANNI BATTISTA CIMA DA CONEGLIANO called CIMA
(c.1495–c1517)
The Incredulity of St. Thomas
Panel, $85 \times 63\frac{1}{2}$ in (216×162 cm)
Gallerie dell' Accademia, Venice

The combined influence of Giovanni Bellini and Mantegna can be seen in this luminously statuesque painting, framed by a classical arch. Cima's work may in some respects be seen as a reaction to the influence of Giorgione, emphasiz- *ing formal relations and shapes against the sky in a manner which contrasts strongly to Giorgione and Titian's more overall approach to pictorial composition. The effect here is almost that of a bas-relief.*

71. JACOPO ZUCCHI (1541–89)
The Treasures of the Sea
Copper, $20\frac{3}{4} \times 17\frac{3}{4}$ in (53 × 45 cm)
Galleria Borghese, Rome

The exotic world of the Mannerists is conspicuously exemplified in this exotic painting, with its wealth of figures, its curious objects and its awareness of those new lands which were being publicized by the explorers of the sixteenth century, thus opening up the frontiers of the European imagination. One cannot imagine what Michelangelo's response might have been to this curious, if logical, development from his idealized heroic nudes.

72. DOMENICO ZAMPIERI called
DOMENICHINO (1581–1641)
The Hunt of Diana
Galleria Borghese, Rome

The Hunt of Diana *takes place in the happy realm of Arcadia and represents a curious fusion of High Renaissance idealism with the rich colour tonalities of Venetian art. Himself a pupil of Raphael, Domenichino also benefitted* from Leonardo's influence in his native Bologna. Thus mixing the traditions of Raphael, Leonardo and Titian, Domenichino's work represents an ideal synthesis of early sixteenth-century art.

IV

Popes and Painters

THE WEALTH OF the Popes, built on the contribution of the faithful, on the sale of indulgences, on shrewd business deals, on such accidents as the discovery of gold mines in the papal states – which produced 100,000 gold ducats a year – was immense, and the occupants of the See of Peter were themselves usually rich men, drawn from the major dynasties of the peninsula. Moreover, as soon as a man became Pope, his relatives automatically became princes who created their own dynasties – the Borghese, the della Rovere, the Farnese, the Borgias, the Colonnas – and they needed their palaces, their paintings, their sumptuous works of art, as did those other princes of the church – the Cardinals. Never before in the history of the world had so many wealthy patrons been concentrated in one city.

As soon as Rome had been established as the sole seat of the papacy at the beginning of the fifteenth century, the Popes organized a programme of renovation and building to create a suitable background for their office. Pope Martin V established workshops for jewellers, embroiderers and goldsmiths, restored churches and employed Masaccio, Pisanello and Gentile da Fabriano. His successor Pope Eugenius IV rebuilt and enlarged the Lateran Palace, and brought Fra Angelico to Rome. Nicholas V employed Piero della Francesca, Fra Angelico and Andrea del Castagno to decorate the palace of the Vatican, and papal agents all over Europe were commissioned to acquire works of art for it. Paul II introduced printing into Rome from Venice, reorganized the university, restored classical monuments, and competed with Lorenzo de' Medici in acquiring works of art. When he died, his collection included forty-seven bronzes, twenty-five portable altars with painted or mosaic backgrounds, many paintings, 400 cameos and intaglios, a great deal of jewellery and a remarkable collection of Byzantine objects in gold and ivory. Francesco della Rovere, who became Sixtus IV in 1471, was not only the most politically ruthless of all the Renaissance Popes, but a patron of artists on a massive scale. He reorganized and rebuilt the Vatican Library, opened up the museum of the Capitol and completed the construction, but not the decoration, of the Sistine Chapel which bears his name. He summoned to Rome, Botticelli, Signorelli, Ghirlandaio, Melozzo da Forlì, Perugino, Verrocchio and Pollaiuolo, and in 1478 founded the Academy of St. Luke to incorporate the thirty artists who were working for him at that time.

1. MICHELANGELO BUONARROTI
(1475–1564)
Christ the Judge
Fresco, 540 × 520 in (1370 × 1320 cm)
Sistine Chapel, Rome

One of the most powerful and unexpected images of Christ in Western art, this figure occupies the centre of the fresco behind the altar and dominates the whole of the Sistine Chapel with its eternal magnificence.

I

It was another della Rovere, Pope Julius II (1503–13), who was responsible for commissioning the greatest works of Raphael and Michelangelo, and for starting the building of the new basilica of St. Peter's which was to dominate not only the city of Rome, but the whole world of European art for centuries to come. He was the organizer of the papal collections which today are housed in the various constituent museums of the Vatican. The *Apollo Belvedere*, the *Laocoön*, *Hercules* and the two allegorical groups of the *Tiber* and the *Nile* were added to the collections in the Belvedere. During his reign, and that of his successor Pope Leo X, Michelangelo completed the paintings in the Sistine chapel and Raphael finished those in the Vatican.

Of the three great artists – all virtually contemporaries – who formed the blazing centre of Renaissance art, and whose impact on the history of painting has been of a unique kind, Leonardo da Vinci was the one who was least affected by the splendour of papal patronage. Indeed, his mind was so lively, his interests so wide-ranging, his curiosity so insatiable that it would have been difficult for him to find in any one place, or any one patron, the scope which his genius instinctively demanded. Admitted to Verrocchio's Florentine studio in 1469 he began to achieve fame as a painter, first as an assistant to Verrocchio and then on his own. He was commissioned by the monks of S. Donato to paint *The Adoration of the Magi*, which he characteristically left unfinished; other works of this period are *The Annunciation* and *St. Jerome*. Deciding to exploit the considerable technical and scientific skills he had acquired, he wrote to Ludovico il Moro, one of the pugnacious Sforza Dukes of Milan, offering his services as a military engineer, but mainly being employed as a painter, sculptor and architect. It was in Milan that he started his *Treatise on Painting* and various other theoretical studies in which he manifested with such brilliance his typically Florentine interest in the nature of life and landscape. The range of his activities was no less remarkable than the range of places he visited. For instance, in the year 1500 he was in Milan in January, in Mantua in February drawing Isabella d'Este; in April he was in Venice advising on the defence of the city against the Turks, and by May he was back in Florence where he stayed until 1506, working on a number of projects – again mostly uncompleted. It was here that he began the *Mona Lisa*.

In the meantime the French had conquered Milan and in 1506, at the invitation of Charles d'Amboise, Leonardo da Vinci moved there and stayed until the French were driven out six years later. Returning to Florence he entered the service of Giuliano de' Medici, one of the sons of Lorenzo, and followed him to Rome when his brother Giovanni became Pope Leo X. Giuliano died in 1515, and Leonardo accepted the invitation of Francis I to move to the French court. He settled in Amboise and died near there in 1519.

Leonardo was not so much a man as a phenomenon. His actual paintings are limited in number, and bear no quantitative relation to the output of his contemporaries. But the impact he made on those who came into contact with him was remarkable, and his restlessly explorative interests brought to landscape and portraiture, new dimensions of significance. In his belief in the unrivalled power of the human intellect to recognize, even if not to solve, problems he was the very epitome of the Renaissance man. Seeking and finding constant analogies between man and nature, he endowed his pupils with an attitude to art which largely transformed it. His concern with the fantastic, moulded the work of Piero di Cosimo, the gently disciplined art of Perugino, the poise and masterly compositional skills of Andrea del Sarto, the mellifluous classicism of Fra Bartolommeo and the lyrical elegance of Sodoma can all be traced to his precepts and practice. Moreover, those developments in style which took place later in the century are more directly attributable to his influence than to that of anyone else.

If Leonardo had immeasurably raised the intellectual status of the artist, then Michelangelo, who belonged by birth to the minor Florentine nobility, did much to improve its social status. He maintained a haughtiness and independence in relation to

2. LEONARDO DA VINCI (1452–1519)
The Adoration of the Magi
Panel, $95\frac{1}{2} \times 96\frac{3}{4}$ in (243×246 cm)
Uffizi, Florence

In March 1481 Leonardo was commissioned to paint an altarpiece for the monks of S. Donato at Scopeto, near Florence, but it never got beyond the stage of this monochrome painting. Despite its unfinished state, the picture is important as a summing up of later fifteenth-century compositional aims.

his patrons, which prefigures the romantic ideal of this relationship which became popular in the nineteenth century. But although Florentine by nature and by training, Michelangelo was made by papal patronage. The fecundity of his creative gifts, the breadth of his imagination and, in contrast to Leonardo, the range and size of his finished works, could only have found scope in a city where so much was being spent on so many stimulating projects.

His first Roman project, the *Pietà* in St. Peter's, was commissioned in 1498, and completed two years later, arousing both admiration and controversy because of the youthful beauty of the Virgin – which he guilefully attributed to her being born without original sin and thus being exempt from the ravages of age. Between 1500 and 1505 he worked in Florence, completing the *David*, the *Madonna* (now in the cathedral

3

at Bruges), the *Madonna* relief (now in the Royal Academy, London) and being commissioned by the Signoria to paint a battle picture for the new council chamber in the Palazzo Vecchio. This was never completed, but it stimulated him into making many drawings – some five hundred of which still exist – thus raising that art form to a status among collectors and connoisseurs which it had never possessed before.

In the spring of 1505 he was summoned to Rome by the ferocious Pope Julius II to make a tomb for him. The two quarrelled incessantly and Michelangelo made sudden escapes to Florence or Bologna, but always returned. The project for the tomb was abandoned and he undertook a new commission, to produce a vast fresco cycle for the barrel vault of the Sistine Chapel. It involved a space measuring 120 × 46 feet (36.5 × 14m), broken by the intersection of windows which create triangular spaces which he filled with figures of the prophets and Sibyls – interesting evidence of the way in which, at that time, classical and Christian ideas were intermingled. Unlike other artists who would have employed a large number of assistants, Michelangelo painted the whole of this huge work himself, working in two spells – the first starting in April 1508 and ending in September 1510; the second stretching from April 1511 until 31

4

3. MICHELANGELO BUONARROTI
(1475–1564)
The Holy Family
Panel, 47 in (120 cm) in diameter
Uffizi, Florence

Painted in 1504 for the marriage of Agnolo Doni and Maddalena Strozzi, this circular panel contains a remarkable concentration of form within a limited area. Its spiral composition and solidity of form are emphasized by the nudes in the background, which forecast those of the Sistine Chapel.

4. RAFFAELLO SANZIO called
RAPHAEL (1483–1520)
Cardinal Bibbiena
Oil on canvas, $26\frac{1}{2} \times 25\frac{1}{2}$ in (68 × 65 cm)
Pitti, Florence

This portrait depicts one of Raphael's most enthusiastic and most deeply learned patrons, Bernardo Dovizi, Cardinal Bibbiena (1470–1520) who had been the tutor of the children of Lorenzo de' Medici.

October 1512, when the whole work was unveiled. He was thirty-seven and he had created what may well be thought of as the greatest individual achievement in the history of European art. Redolent of that *terribilità* which was considered to be one of the hallmarks of his genius, it displayed an unrivalled knowledge of human anatomy, a dazzling command of compositional skill, and a magnificence of conception which were perfectly attuned to the glory of the new papal Rome which was being created by a succession of ambitious pontifs.

Architecture was his next preoccupation, and after designing the Medici Chapel and the Laurentian Library in Florence, he returned to Rome in 1534, where he worked for the rest of his life. His first great commission was to paint *The Last Judgment* behind the altar in the Sistine Chapel, which was unveiled exactly twenty years after the paintingso n the ceilings. More sombre in feeling, more terrible in its dark intensities it reflected not only his own new concern with religion, but the horrors of Charles V's invasion of Italy, which had humbled the pride of both Florence and Rome. In one of his sonnets he expressed this new sense of anguish:

'Né pinger né scolpir fia più che quieti
L'anima volta a quell 'Amor divine
Ch'asperse a prender noi, 'n croce le bracchia.'[1]

('Neither painting nor sculpture can quieten the soul which is turned to Divine Love, which to embrace us, opened wide His arms on the Cross'.)

The last thirty-four years of his long life were mainly devoted to the completion of the new basilica of St. Peter (which had been started by Bramante) and was to be finished half a century after his death, altered considerably from his original conception but owing a great deal to it.

Raphael owed as much to Rome and the papacy as Michelangelo did, but he was far less intransigent and more concerned with establishing a mode of creativity than with spurring himself on to frenzies of inspiration. More than any other artist he converted all that had been achieved in art between 1450 and his own early death at the early age of thirty-seven in 1520, into a system which was to be the basis of academic art in Europe for the next four centuries. 'He always did what others dreamed of doing', said Goethe, and for Michelangelo's *terribilità* he substituted a *mirabile giudizio* or wonderful judgment, more within the reach of the many of his contemporaries and successors who saw him as the paragon of art.

A pupil of Perugino, his move to Florence in 1504 brought him into contact with the work of Leonardo, whose influence is strong in the *Madonna del Granduca*, and whose example gave his work a gentle elegance which it was always to retain. In 1508, he was summoned to Rome by Julius II to decorate the *Stanze*, the old apartments of the previous Pope in the Vatican, on which Luca Signorelli, Bartolommeo, Bramantino and Sodoma had been working. He first decorated the *Stanza della Segnatura*, then the *Stanza d'Eliodoro*, in which he included the Pope's portrait, and finally the *Stanza dell' Incendio*, which he completed in 1517. Unlike Michelangelo, he employed assistants, notably Giulio Romano, but the scale of these Vatican murals is nonetheless incredibly impressive. At the same time he was showered with commissions from Roman notables. For the Sienese banker Agostino Chigi he decorated the Villa Farnesina, and in 1516 he sketched the decorations for Cardinal Bibbiena's bathroom at the Vatican – a remarkable exercise in erotic art. For Giuliano de' Medici he designed the Villa Madama, and supervized the decoration of the Vatican *logge* in a style which has left its imprint on the history of European design. In 1518 he was appointed supervisor of all the works at the Vatican, and was commissioned to design ten tapestries to be hung on the walls of the Sistine Chapel underneath Michelangelo's frescoes. These, based on the lives of the Apostles, were woven in Brussels and delivered to the Vatican in 1519. So enthusiastically were they received that the cartoons were lent first to the Duke of Mantua, to have a set made, and then to the Duke of Urbino. In the seventeenth century they were acquired by Charles I of England, and now hang in the Victoria and Albert Museum in London. That naturalism and ability to react to others' personalities which is so apparent in the figures of the Swiss Guards in *The Mass of Bolsena* made him also a portraitist of great skill and persuasive veracity. Widely appreciated by scholars and statesmen, by bankers and ordinary citizens of Rome, he belonged to the world of Castiglione's *Courtier*, and the artistic capital which he left behind was exploited shamelessly by his followers.

5. TIZIANO VECELLI called TITIAN
(*c*.1487–1576)
John the Baptist
Oil on canvas, 79 × 52½ in (201 × 134 cm)
Gallerie dell' Accademia, Venice

This magnificent life-painting, simple, direct and dramatic, reveals the extent to which Titian's gifts were based on a solid foundation of draughtsmanship. The treatment of the landscape shows a typical Venetian romanticism.

5

Raphael's work showed not only the influence of Leonardo, but quite noticeably that of the Venetians who, during this period, were dominated by the massive reputation and achievement of Titian, whose long life spanned most of the sixteenth century. Titian received his training in the studio of Giovanni Bellini (1430–1516), and the *Pietà*, which he was in the process of painting for his own tomb when he died, was finished by his pupil, Palma Giovane, who died in 1628. Less concerned with the kind of philosophical and religious symbolism which exercized the minds of artists as disparate as Botticelli and Raphael, he united a strong feeling for simple, strong colours, with the dramatic siting of figures against a background of light. His attitude to the human figure was more realistic than that of Giorgione, to whose art his own owed much, and he was arguably one of the greatest painters of the nude the world has known, with an incredible skill in using luminous colour to describe the quality of skin.

Although changes in an artist's style cannot be entirely ascribed to shifts in patronage, there can be little doubt that the most significant point in Titian's development, when he changed over to a greater monumentality of expression, was when he had become so famous that his main patrons were no longer the affluent merchant princes of Venice, but the Pope and the Emperor. In 1533 he was appointed court painter to the Holy Roman Emperor, the Hapsburg Charles V, and began a series of portraits of all the notabilities of his time; Cardinal Ippolito de' Medici, the Duke and Duchess of Urbino, Cardinal Pietro Bembo, and Pietro Aretino. Around 1545 he was invited to Rome (of which he was made a Citizen) to stay with Pope Paul III at the Vatican, where he painted members of the Farnese family.

After a brief visit to Florence in 1547 he went on to Augsburg to work at the Imperial Court, painting several portraits of the Emperor and his son Philip II, who for the remaining years of the painter's life was his most devoted patron. At the end of his years he fell very much under the influence of Michelangelo, and at the same time reverted to the more emotional colours and feelings of his early works. Profound though Titian's influence was on the art of painting in oils, and few who came after him could ever disregard it, even greater was his significance as an international figure and the effects it had on the social status of the artist and indeed of art itself. Nobody before had painted so many popes, emperors and kings; nobody had been received at so many courts almost as a prince rather than as a painter. He anticipated the career of an artist who greatly admired him, the Fleming, Rubens who was later to receive the same kind of Imperial patronage, and he emphasized the cosmopolitan prestige which Italian art now possessed. Dürer's contacts with it for instance had been consistent and important for his art. His first visit had taken place in 1494, his second to Venice in 1505. In the period between 1500 and 1507 he studied Mantegna's engravings very closely, and received instructions from Jacopo de Barbari, one of the latter's pupils who was typical of those harbingers of the new Italian style. Born in Venice, Barbari worked for the Emperor Maximilian, Frederick the Wise of Saxony, Philip of Burgundy and Margaret of Austria, and so brought to Germany, Saxony, Austria and the Netherlands something of the excitement, the novelty and the glamour of Italian art.

What had been happening in Florence and Rome was soon transmitted to other centres, where it was grafted onto local traditions. In Parma, for instance, Correggio who had been brought up under the influence of Mantegna, and then succumbed to some of Leonardo's mannerisms, had never visited Rome, but possessed an intimate knowledge of the works of Raphael and Michelangelo. This knowledge was gained presumably through prints and drawings which were being circulated throughout Italy, a significant indication of the new speed and ease with which styles and mannerisms could be communicated in an age in which developments in the craft of papermaking and of engraving had given graphic media a new importance. Correggio spent most of his working life in Parma, where he displayed hitherto unmatched skills in perspective effects, seen in his paintings of domes and ceilings, which give an

6

6. ALBRECHT DÜRER (1471–1528)
Portrait of his Father
Panel, $18\frac{1}{2} \times 15\frac{1}{4}$ in (47×39 cm)
Uffizi, Florence

Painted when he was about nineteen, this is one of the two portraits Dürer did of his father; the other is in the National Gallery, London. It shows how soon this young artist had found a purely individual style for himself, full of penetration, mastery of colour, and compositional simplicity and directness.

impression of being open to the sky, with the figures seen from below in the process of flight. All his works are marked by an intense, lyrical fervour and ecstacy which anticipate the religious fervours of the seventeenth century. Similar qualities are to be found in the works of many other provincial artists of the same period. For example, Dosso Dossi of Ferrara came under the influence of Giorgione, Titian and Correggio, but made a personal contribution in his mysterious, exotic landscapes which have a curiously romantic quality.

The changes which had taken place in the later works of Titian and of Michelangelo, and the new emphasis on feeling apparent in the works of painters of a younger generation such as Correggio and Dosso Dossi, were indicative of a new intellectual climate which was related to things which were happening in the wider world of politics. Rich and powerful though they had been in contrast to feudal monarchies of northern Europe, the Italian states were virtually helpless when faced with the great centralized monarchies, with their huge resources, their sophisticated weapons, their endless supplies of manpower. The rivalry between Francis I of France and the Emperor Charles V was fought out on the plains of northern Italy, and when the latter triumphed at the battle of Pavia (1525) his army, many of whom were Lutherans, marched on Rome and put it to sack with incredible brutality. Even though a political settlement was reached between Charles and Clement VII at Bologna in 1530, the independence of the small states of Italy was at an end. Political problems were compounded by religious ones. The Renaissance popes had apparently raised the papacy to a position of splendour, yet by the mid-sixteenth century most of Europe had broken free from direct papal control, either by founding national churches, as in England, or, as was the case in France, by establishing a concordat rigorously limiting papal power. Inevitably a reaction set in, as the Church realized how embattled it was. In 1542 the Holy Office or Inquisition was set up; in 1543 the *Index Librorum Prohibitorum* introduced censorship, and in 1545, the Council of Trent began those deliberations which were to transform over the next few decades the nature of the church, and even of the papacy.

The full effect of these responses by Rome, and their influence on the arts would not be felt until the seventeenth century, but by the middle of the fifteenth, a whole nexus of stylistic attitudes had grown up, different both from those of the Renaissance which preceded them, and the Baroque which followed them, and which are usefully grouped together under the label of Mannerism. Some of its characteristics involved attitudes, some stylistic devices, some subject matter. There was an almost hysterical emphasis on originality of inspiration, often stimulating an interest in the exotic or the bizarre. Figures were elongated or distorted; disconcerting elements were introduced; colours were often strident or discordant, with an emphasis on bright pinks, blues, acidulous greens and light yellows; lighting became theatrically dramatic. In terms of composition there was a strong emphasis on sinuous, writhing rhythms, serpentine lines and a general, almost neurotic sense of vertiginous instability. Although artists such as Pontormo, Bronzino and Nicolo dell'Abbate saw themselves as the heirs of the great masters of the Renaissance, carrying on the legacy of Michelangelo and Raphael, and although they sought an ideal beauty superior to that to be found in mere natural phenomena, they were in effect partly undermining the rational empiricism which had marked painting during the previous two centuries. It was an assertion of the romantic as opposed to the classical attitude, and it is interesting that artists such as Domenico Beccafumi, a Sienese artist whose works showed the bright, decorative artistic traditions of that city, was also influenced by Dürer. So too was Pontormo, one of the first painters in whose works a strong, neurotic element is clearly discernible, reflected in a certain irrationality of composition, swirling exaggerated figures and colours which verge on the hysterical. Nor are these characteristics entirely fanciful. When he was at work on the church of San Lorenzon Florence he kept a diary, part of which has survived, and the following extract shows that hypochondria and attendant symptoms of *angst* are not peculiar to the twentieth century:

'Wednesday I did the rest of the cupid, and had to stoop uncomfortably all day, so that on Thursday I had a pain in my kidneys; on Friday, apart from the pain I was ill-disposed, and did not feel well, so I had no supper that night; on the morning of the same day which was the 29th March (1555) I did the hand and half the arm of Saint Lawrence, and the knee and part of the leg on which his hand rests; in the evening I ate nothing. I had no food till Saturday night, when I ate ten ounces of bread, two eggs and a borage salad. On Sunday the 31st I had lunch in the house of Daniello, fish and capon. In the evening I had no meal, and on Monday I was distracted by pains in my body, I got up, but owing to the wind and the cold, I returned to bed and stayed there till six o'clock, and felt ill all day. In the evening I supped on a little boiled meat, with beets and butter, and I remained thus, not knowing what was the matter with me. I think my going back to bed must have harmed me, yet now at four o'clock in the morning I feel much better.'[2]

His fear of death was notorious among his contemporaries. He worked in a studio the only entrance to which was up a ladder, attached to a pulley, which he used to draw up after him.

Pontormo was a batchelor, but he adopted Bronzino as his son, a man whose art verged on elegant decadence rather than on the outright neurotic, and some of whose paintings might almost belong to the period of Art Nouveau, so artfully contrived are their postures, their arabesques of form, so emphatic is their assurance. In portraiture especially, his work breathes a disdainful objectivity, a cool detachment. The same Beardsley-like elegance is apparent in the works of Raphael's main pupil and assistant Giulio Romano, who also specialized in erotic prints and overwhelming effects, such as

7. ANTONIO CORREGGIO (1489–1534)
The Virgin Adoring the Child Jesus
Oil on canvas, $31\frac{3}{4} \times 26\frac{1}{4}$ in (81×67 cm)
Uffizi, Florence

Correggio painted this picture in about 1520, when he was very much under the influence of Leonardo. The dramatic *effect of the lighting is especially noteworthy and the sheer delight of the Virgin in her Child.*

8

8. AGNOLO BRONZINO (1503–72)
Portrait of Lucrezia Panciatichi
Panel, 40¾ × 33 in (104 × 85 cm)
Uffizi, Florence

The extraordinary physical beauty of this Florentine woman is enhanced by the vivid colours of her dress, the interplay of textures and the sombre background from which she emerges. Bronzino was one of the most important portrait painters of the Mannerist period, but his religious pictures are usually criticized on the grounds that they are devoid of any kind of feeling and simply exercises in elegant physical attenuation.

9. JACOPO TINTORETTO (1518–94)
The Deposition
Oil on canvas, 89¼ × 115½ in (227 × 294 cm)
Gallerie dell' Accademia, Venice

Originally painted for the church of L'Umilita in Venice, Tintoretto's dramatically moving image of the taking down of Christ from the cross has all the poignancy and dramatic intensity which the age of the Council of Trent demanded.

the gigantic paintings in the Palazzo del Te in Mantua.

There was indeed a strong erotic undercurrent to much Mannerist art, which may well have been one of the reasons why it became a leading Italian export in the latter half of the sixteenth century. Niccolo dell' Abbate, who was born in Modena (but achieved his personal style under the tuition of Parmigianino (who had fled to Bologna from Rome after the sack of that city and whose style combined a typical Mannerist elegance and movement with considerable interest in landscape), spent most of his working life in France where he carried out extensive decoration at Fontainebleau and painted numerous pictures of Charles IX, which did much to create that French school of painting which found its finest expression in the works of Claude and Poussin. His figure paintings were richly sensuous, but his landscapes, romantic, dramatically conceived, showing traces of Flemish influence are especially interesting. Another

9

Italian artist, Rosso Fiorentino, also worked at Fontainebleau from 1530 until his death in 1540, and had possibly a greater influence than dell' Abbate because so many of his works appeared in the form of engravings. The spirit of Mannerism touched even those artists who did not succumb to its more violent manifestations – in Spain, El Greco, in Italy Tintoretto and Veronese. The occasional distortions, the sense of the unexpected, the dramatic effects of light and shade, the daring compositional effects which characterize so many of Tintoretto's works are clear signs of this. So too is the religious intensity which marks works such as *The Deposition*. But underlying all this there are clear signs of that Venetian vernacular which he had inherited from Titian, and to which he contributed so much. His work was even more solidly rooted in his native city than that of any of his illustrious predecessors. He never ventured outside the dominions of the Republic, and relied for patronage entirely on the *Scuole* and the City Fathers whose commissions allowed him to maintain a large workshop with numerous assistants. His works are characterized by enormous energy, by an innate sensuality far removed from the eroticism of those painters who practised the more superficial techniques of Mannerism. His oblique compositions and sinuous figures impress with their vitality rather than their elaborate sophistication, and his portraits convey a greater feeling of intensity because of their sombre backgrounds. He converted the Mannerist manipulation of perspective from the theatrical into the dramatic, refining the actual technique of oil painting by a new use of rough brush-stroke which caught facets of light, adding to his works a kind of sparkle which had never been seen before.

10

10. PAOLO VERONESE (*c.*1528–88)
The Battle of Lepanto
Detail of an oil on canvas, $66\frac{1}{2} \times 53\frac{3}{4}$ in
(169×137 cm)
Gallerie dell' Accademia, Venice

Painted c.1571 to commemorate the battle of that year in   commanded by Don John of Austria, this is one of the
which the Turks were defeated by a Christian fleet   greatest testaments to Venetian patriotism.

Manneristic tendencies were more apparent in the work of his contemporary, Veronese, whose output was enormous, though he himself never left Venice. He had at his disposition every trick which an astonishing technical virtuosity could command, and was deluged with commissions which drew out of him all those elements of magnificence and decorative splendour which characterize his genius. He was in a sense the heir of Gentile Bellini in his ability to encapsulate the splendours of Venice, and the ancestor of Tiepolo in his command of luscious clear colour, sensuous figure painting and spectacular effects. He lived in a Venice which seemed to be losing its earlier religious intensities, and even his treatment of sacred subjects is tinged with a kind of pagan classicism. The church authorities were conscious of this and in 1573 he was summoned before the Inquisition for having introduced too many profane themes into his painting of *Christ in the House of Levi*. It was a significant happening, portending the end of Mannerism, indicating the imminence of yet another change in the cultural climate. The Mannerist period had been a curious episode in the history of art and Eric Mercer has summed it up admirably:

> 'It was an art which showed, both by its slavish copying, and its wilful defiance of the canons of the past its deep roots in the Italian Renaissance. It was simultaneously rigidly disciplined, and wilfully licentious, elegant and *farouche*, pornographic and ecstatically religious, lost in the "other world" of antiquity, and yet vividly conscious of the horrors of the sixteenth century. It was the art of men of splendid talents and a glorious tradition, robbed of their heritage by the necessities and accidents of European history, at the very moment they were about to enter upon it. It was the art of a tortured and often despairing society.'[3]

11

11. BERNARDINO PINTURICCHIO
(c. 1454–1513)
Alexander VI
Detail of a fresco, 148 × 151½ in (376 × 385 cm)
Borgia Appartments in the Sala dei Misteri,
Musei Vaticani, Rome

The convincing realism of this portrait of one of the most famous Renaissance popes reflects the new sense of perception of individual human personality which was one of the main philosophical revelations of the Renaissance. It is a detail from a larger work depicting the Resurrection. Christ's tomb can be seen on the right.

12. GIOVANNI ANTONIO BAZZI
called IL SODOMA (1477–49)
St. Sebastian
Oil on canvas, 81 × 60½ in (206 × 154 cm)
Pitti, Florence

Sodoma, whose frescoes are a good deal more old-fashioned in style than his paintings on canvas and panel, brought to Siena the influence of Leonardo, and foreshadowed the coming of Mannerism.

12

13

13. IL SODOMA
The Holy Family
Panel, $29\frac{1}{2} \times 26\frac{1}{4}$ in (75 × 67 cm)
Galleria Borghese, Rome

There is a touching intimacy about the way in which St. Joseph is offering a flower to the Child Jesus, who is smiling *affectionately at him. The landscape in the top right-hand corner of the painting is especially interesting.*

14. LODOVICO MAZZOLINO
(*c.*1480–*c.*1528)
The Incredulity of St. Thomas
Panel, $11\frac{3}{4} \times 7\frac{3}{4}$ in (30 × 20 cm)
Galleria Borghese, Rome

The mere fact that the artist has not fully mastered the art of figure-painting gives the foreground a special kind of charm, which is accentuated by the extreme complexity of Christ's *halo. The background, however, with its air of fantasy, is reminiscent of the Surrealist buildings of the Neapolitan artist Monsu' Desiderio.*

15

16

15. GIOVANNI GIROLAMO SAVOLDO (fl.1508–48)
Portrait of a Youth
Oil on canvas, 23½ × 15¾ in (60 × 40 cm)
Galleria Borghese, Rome

The slightly melancholic look on the young man's face, the position of his hand and the structuring of his dress make this painting highly typical of Savoldo's portraiture which are also noted for their light effects.

16. LORENZO LOTTO (c.1480–1556)
Portrait of a Gentleman in his Study
Oil on canvas, 38½ × 43½ in (98 × 111 cm)
Gallerie dell' Accademia, Venice

Combining elements of still-life to enhance the effects of portraiture, this work reveals Lotto's delicate pictorial sensibilities. It also typifies in its subject the new kind of virtuoso created by the Renaissance; a man interested in music, literature, the fine arts, natural science (note the lizard) and other facets of learning.

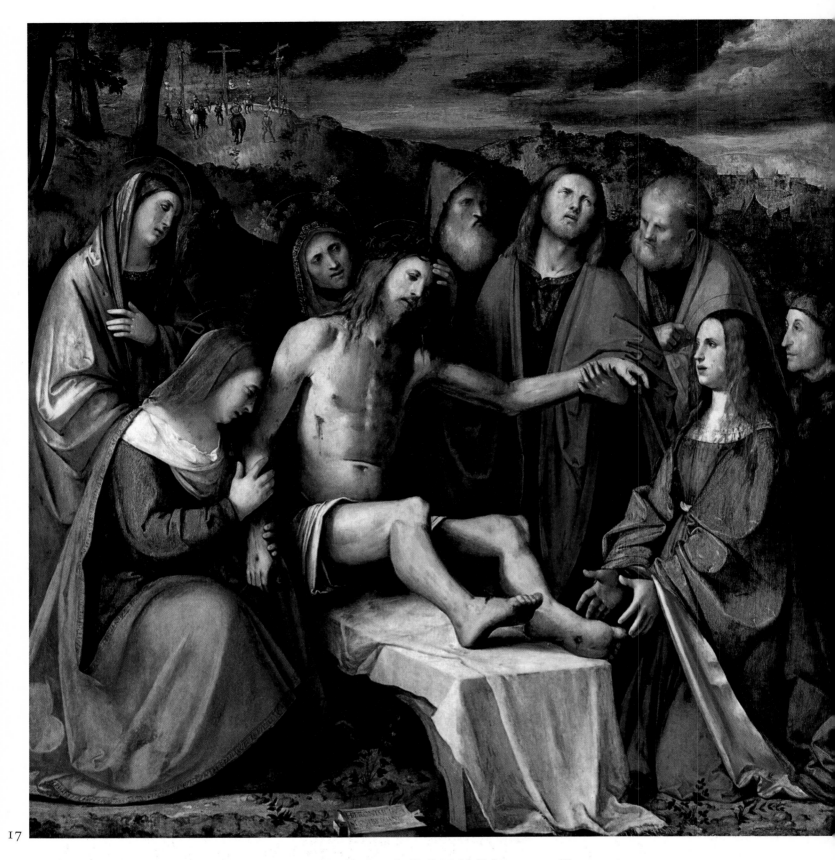

17

17. GIROLAMO ROMANI known as IL ROMANINO (*c.*1484–1544)
The Deposition of Christ
Panel, 72 × 72¾ in (183 × 185 cm)
Gallerie dell' Accademia, Venice

This painting is dated 1510 and is the earliest known work of the artist. It is marked by strongly Titianesque qualities, *although in the arrangement of the figures and the profiles there are suggestions of an earlier attitude.*

19

18. RAFFAELLO SANZIO called
RAPHAEL (1483–1520)
The Miracle of the Mass at Bolsena
Detail of a fresco, $185\frac{1}{2} \times 280\frac{1}{4}$ in (471×712 cm)
Musei Vaticani, Rome

Between 1512 and 1514 Raphael was at work on decorating the Stanze d'Eliodoro in the Vatican, the general theme being the defence of the spiritual and territorial integrity of the papacy. The Miracle of the Mass at Bolsena *covered one of the smaller walls and other subjects were the* Liberation of St. Peter *and the* Expulsion of Heliodorus.

19. SEBASTIANO DEL PIOMBO
(*c*.1485–1547)
The Death of Adonis
Oil on canvas, $74\frac{1}{4} \times 116$ in (189×295 cm)
Uffizi, Florence

Sebastiano's Venetian upbringing is reflected in the landscape, part of which suggests one of the islands in the Venetian lagoon, such as Murano. The figures and the theme are, however, Roman in feeling.

20

20. GIOVANNI ANTONIO
PORDENONE (1484–1539)
Judith
Oil on canvas, $37\frac{1}{4} \times 30\frac{1}{2}$ in (95 × 78 cm)

The smouldering intensity of this painting is suggestive of those effects of light and shade of which Rembrandt was to make himself master a century or so later. Pordonone's especial mastery of spatial relationships is also apparent.

21

21. DOMENICO BECCAFUMI
(1486–1551)
The Holy Family with St. John
Panel, 34½ in (88 cm) in diameter
Pitti, Florence

Although he was influenced by Sodoma and the Floren-
tines, Beccafumi's style still reflects his Sienese origins and
background. A member of the High Renaissance generation
in Rome, his work is known for its intensity of emotion.

22

23

24

22. BONIFAZIO DE' PITATI known as
BONIFAZIO VERONESE (1487–1553)
The Banquet of Dives
Oil on canvas, 80¼ × 171½ in (204 × 436 cm)
Gallerie dell' Accademia, Venice

The idyllic tradition of Giorgione converted into a more *the fêtes champêtres of Watteau and the delightful*
social context gives this painting a quality which forecasts *melancholy of later romanticism.*

23. BONIFAZIO VERONESE
Sacred Conversation Piece
Panel, 42 × 57 in (107 × 145 cm)
Pitti, Florence

This is a typical Venetian painting in the richness of the *warmth of feeling. The faces of the two donors have a*
colouring, the beauty of the distant landscape and its general *Flemish quality and note the accuracy of the globe.*

24. TIZIANO VECELLI called TITIAN
(1488–1576)
Venus Bandaging Cupid
Oil on canvas, 46¼ × 72¾ in (118 × 185 cm)
Galleria Borghese, Rome

Painted when he was about seventy, this beautiful picture *and his powers of composition until the end. The reflective*
shows the extent to which Titian retained his sense of colour *look on the face of the cupid behind Venus is very subtle.*

25. TITIAN
Pietà
Oil on canvas, 138½ × 137¼ in (352 × 349 cm)
Galleria dell' Accademia, Venice

Intended for his own burial place in the church of the Frari in Venice, this majestic painting was left unfinished by Titian when he died. It was completed by Palma Giovane (1544–1628), *the grand-nephew of Palma Vecchio, who had entered Titian's studio in 1570. The lighting effects have a complex mystery about them.*

26

26. TITIAN
The Englishman
Oil on canvas, $43\frac{1}{2} \times 37\frac{1}{2}$ in (111×96 cm)
Pitti, Florence

The generally accepted title of this painting is based on the *might be a portrait of Guidobaldo da Montefeltro. This is*
man's appearance, although it has been suggested that it *generally considered to be Titian's finest male portrait.*

27. TITIAN
The Presentation of the Virgin
Oil on canvas, 131¾ × 305 in (335 × 775 cm)
Gallerie dell' Accademia, Venice

Painted between 1534 and 1538, this huge composition with its many figures, its contrasting architectural and natural landscapes and overwhelming sense of magnificence, reflects Titian's response to the rising tides of Mannerism.

28. TITIAN
Sacred and Profane Love
Oil on canvas, 46¼ × 109¾ in (118 × 279 cm)
Galleria Borghese, Rome

Although this title was not given to the painting until the end of the seventeenth century, the theme was a familiar one during the Renaissance and no doubt corresponds to the artist's intentions. Stylistically, the painting represents the union of the classicism of Rome with the warm, romantic lyricism of Venice.

29

29. TITIAN
Portrait of Vincenzo Mosti
Oil on canvas, 33 × 26 in (84 × 66 cm)
Pitti, Florence

This portrait of 1526 is unusual for Titian in its predominantly cool, silvery tonality which forms a contrast to his usual warm colours. The rendering of the fabric textures is typical of Titian's sumptuous approach.

30. TITIAN
Cardinal Ippolito de' Medici
Oil on canvas, 54¼ × 41½ in (138 × 106 cm)
Pitti, Florence

This painting shows Titian at his most magnificent. The warm unifying colours, the keen observation of character and the sense of personal self-containment in the face, are all indications of his immense powers as a portraitist.

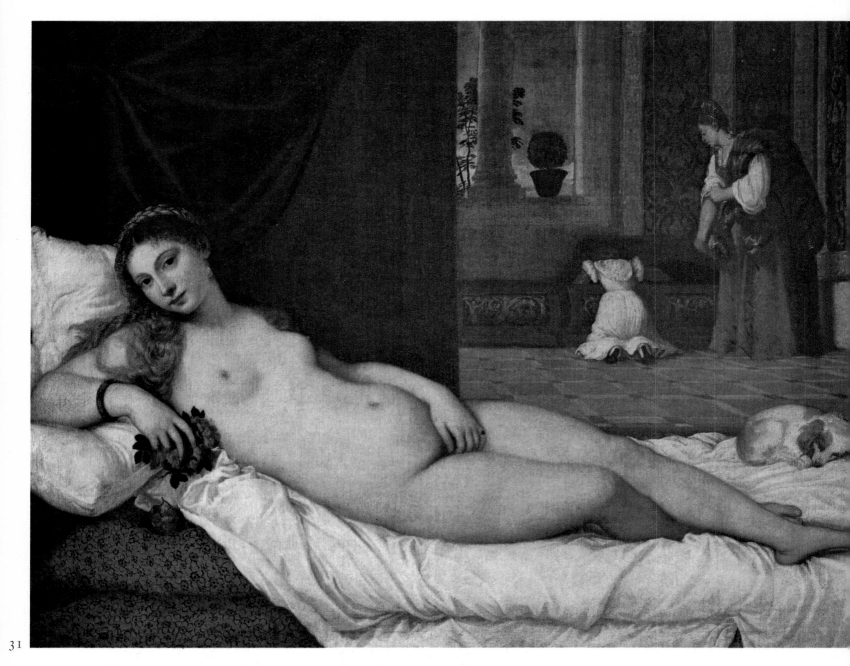

31

31. TITIAN
The Venus of Urbino
Oil on canvas, $46\frac{3}{4} \times 64\frac{3}{4}$ in (119×165 cm)
Uffizi, Florence

Painted in 1538 for Guidobaldo II, Duke of Urbino, this is one of the most famous nude paintings in history. It is a work of Titian's maturity and the very epitome of all that his style stood for. The painting was widely emulated.

32. DOSSO DOSSI (*c.*1489–1542)
Apollo and Daphne
Oil on canvas, $76\frac{1}{4} \times 46\frac{3}{4}$ in (194×119 cm)
Galleria Borghese, Rome

Painted in the first half of the sixteenth century this dramatic work seems to anticipate by a century the fervours and drama of the Baroque. Daphne's metamorphosis into a laurel tree was a highly popular theme during this period.

32

33

33. DOSSO DOSSI
Circe
Oil on canvas, $69\frac{1}{4} \times 68\frac{1}{2}$ in (176×174 cm)
Galleria Borghese, Rome

Connected with a whole range of astrological, mythological and philosophical beliefs, this remarkable painting has attracted the attention of many commentators, none of whom has come to any definitive explanation of its total meaning.

34. ANTONIO CORREGGIO
(*c.*1494–1534)
La Danaë
Oil on canvas, $63\frac{1}{4} \times 76$ in (161 × 193 cm)
Galleria Borghese, Rome

This painting shows to great effect that soft painterly style developed by Correggio and later acclaimed by eighteenth-century art lovers as morbidezza. *A popular mythological heroine in sixteenth and seventeenth-century Italian art,*

Danaë was the daughter of Acrisius, King of Argos, who imprisoned her in a bronze tower. During her captivity she was visited by Zeus in the form of a shower of gold and subsequently gave birth to Perseus.

35

35. ANTONIO CORREGGIO
Repose on the Flight into Egypt
Oil on canvas, $48\frac{1}{4} \times 41\frac{1}{2}$ in (123×106 cm)
Uffizi, Florence

In comparison with the preceding painting by Correggio *composition is more complex and the landscape more*
this picture has a more marked linear quality; the *precisely observed.*

36

36. FRANCESCO D' UMBERTINO
called BACHIACCA (1494–1557)
A Story of Joseph
Panel, $10 \times 5\frac{1}{2}$ in (26×14 cm)
Galleria Borghese, Rome

Part of a series depicting the life of the Old Testament hero Joseph, this episode recounts the story of the stolen cup in a manner which combines the simple directness of popular art with the gestures and colours of sophisticated sources.

37. JACOPO DA PONTORMO
(1494–1557)
The Supper at Emmaus
Panel, $90\frac{1}{2} \times 68\frac{3}{4}$ in (230×175 cm)
Uffizi, Florence

Painted in 1525 for the Charterhouse of Val d'Ema, this finely composed work, with its wealth of detailed observation, suggests the influence both of Dürer's prints and the work of Andrea del Sarto.

38. JACOPO DA PONTORMO
The Martyrs of the Theban Legion
Panel, $26\frac{1}{4} \times 28\frac{1}{2}$ in (67×73 cm)
Pitti, Florence

According to legend, a whole legion from Thebes was crucified on the orders of the Emperor Diocletian (seated in the centre of the picture) for having become Christians. The Mannerist feeling is apparent in the rather bizarre groups of figures and the mildly acidulous colouring which are typical of the increasingly attenuated art of the period.

39. ROSSO FIORENTINO (1495–1540)
Madonna and Saints
Panel, $137\frac{1}{2} \times 102$ in (350×259 cm)
Pitti, Florence

Signed and dated 1522, this picture was painted for the church of Santo Spirito in Florence, and found its way into the Pitti in the early eighteenth century. The influence of Raphael is apparent in the spacious composition with its architectural background. The face of the Child Jesus is rather unfortunate.

38

39

40. FRANCESCO D' UMBERTINO
called BACHIACCA (1497–1557)
St. Mary Magdalene
Panel, 20 × 16½ in (51 × 42 cm)
Pitti, Florence

Bachiacca has chosen to portray the Magdalene as the very and elaborately plaited hair. In her hand she holds the epitome of a late Renaissance courtesan with her rich furs alabaster vase from which she poured oil on Christ's feet.

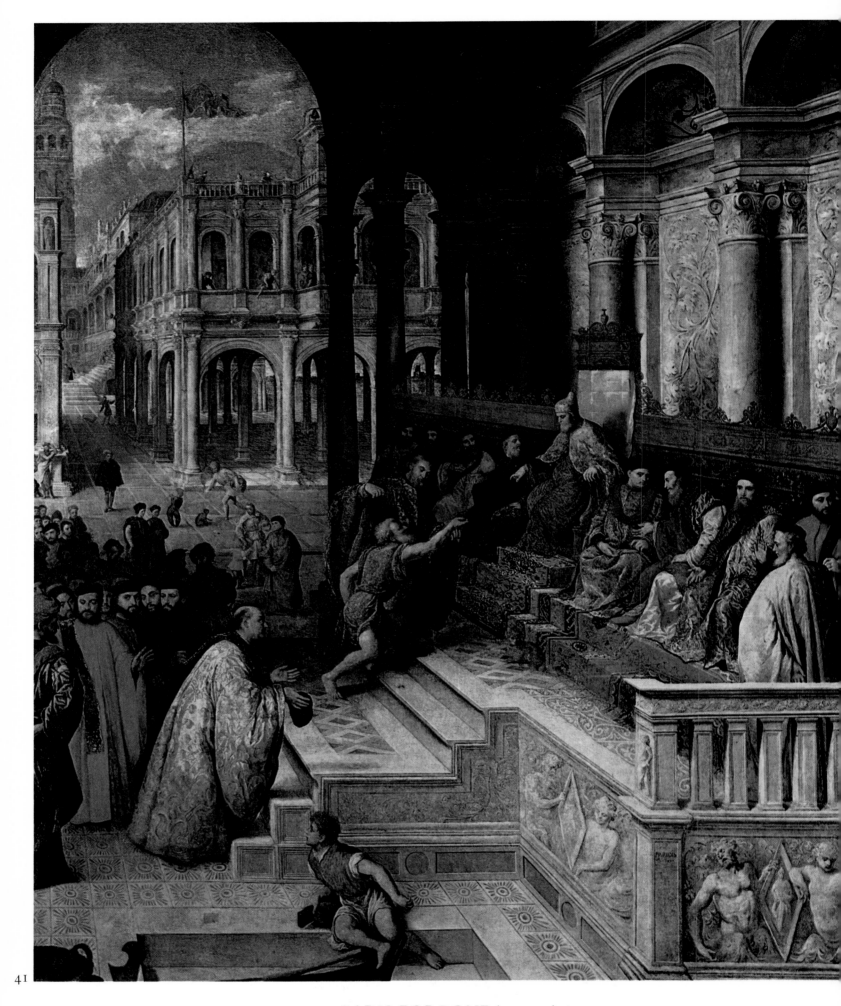

41

41. PARIS BORDONE (1500–71)
The Ceremony of the Ring
Oil on canvas, $145\frac{1}{2} \times 118$ in (370×300 cm)
Gallerie dell' Accademia, Venice

Within a slightly fanciful representation of the courtyard of the Doge's Palace, Bordone shows the moment when a fisherman returns the golden ring cast annually by the Doge into the sea.

42

42. AGNOLO BRONZINO (1503–72)
The Dead Christ
Panel, $41\frac{1}{4} \times 39\frac{1}{4}$ in (105 × 100 cm)
Uffizi, Florence

There is a certain severity in the composition of this Mannerist version of the Pietà, despite the strong emotion on the faces of the Virgin and Mary Magdalene and the glowering background landscape.

43

43. AGNOLO BRONZINO
St. John the Baptist in the Desert
Panel, 47 × 36 in (120 × 92 cm)
Galleria Borghese, Rome

There is an undeniable sexuality about this image of the young St. John with his muscularity and virtual nakedness. *Stylistically, the painting owes a clear debt to Bronzino's master, Pontormo.*

44. AGNOLO BRONZINO
Portrait of Guidobaldo della Rovere
Panel, 44¾ × 33¾ in (114 × 86 cm)
Pitti, Florence

The very epitome of the Renaissance gallant, with his ostentatious cod-piece, damascened armour and obedient *hound, Guidobaldo surveys the world with an air of remote and worldly disdain.*

44

45

45. FRANCESCO PARMIGIANINO
(1505–40)
The Madonna of S. Zavvaria
Panel, $28\frac{1}{2} \times 23\frac{1}{2}$ in (73×60 cm)
Uffizi, Florence

Painted in Bologna in 1528 after a long stay in Rome, this *of the Mannerist approach to religious commissions of*
painting epitomizes all the grace and decorative virtuosity *which Parmigianino was an especially sensitive master.*

47

46. FRANCESCO PARMIGIANINO
*Madonna and Angels (The Madonna with the
Long Neck)*
Panel, $85 \times 51\frac{3}{4}$ in (216×132 cm)
Uffizi, Florence

This painting is the supreme example of the Mannerist style, with its elongations, the use of serpentine lines in its *composition and the feeling of almost a decadent elegance. The work was commissioned in 1548 for a church in Parma.*

47. NICCOLÒ DELL' ABATE (*c.*1512–71)
Landscape
Oil on canvas, $45\frac{1}{2} \times 62\frac{1}{2}$ in (116×159 cm)
Galleria Borghese, Rome

The elongated figures, the quick nervous brush-strokes and the elements of fantasy in the landscape combined with architecture, all suggest the mood of imaginative license which informed so much of the art and literature of the *sixteenth century. Like an episode from some Shakespearean play, these figures seem involved in a strange happening. The sense of the unusual is heightened by the shattered tree-trunks.*

48

48. NICOLÒ DELL' ABATE
Portrait of a Lady
Parchment, $17\frac{3}{4} \times 11\frac{3}{4}$ in (45×30 cm)
Galleria Borghese, Rome

Painted on parchment in the tradition of the miniaturists, this unusual portrait has none of the harshness which that particular technique often involved. The whole work glows with an inner radiance.

49

50

51

49. JACOPO DA PONTE called
BASSANO (*c.*1510–92)
Adam and Eve
Panel, $59\frac{3}{4} \times 29\frac{1}{2}$ in (152×75 cm)
Pitti, Florence

This is a new concept of the Biblical story – relaxed, hedonistic and with a touch of decadent self-indulgence. Jacopo was the most important member of a whole family of Venetian painters and was a pupil of Bonifazio de' Pitati.

As his robust personal style developed, he increasingly sought the opportunity to paint religious subjects into which animals could be incorporated, as can be seen in the head of the calf which protrudes on the left.

50. BASSANO
St. Jerome
Oil on canvas, $46\frac{3}{4} \times 60\frac{1}{2}$ in (119×154 cm)
Gallerie dell' Accademia, Venice

Always retaining something of his peasant ancestry, Bassano combined a strong sense of realism with a delight in

presenting, as in this work, a brightly lit figure against a dark and mysteriously confused background.

51. BASSANO
The Last Supper
Oil on canvas, 66×106 in (168×270 cm)
Galleria Borghese, Rome

The fertility of Bassano's imagination is clearly shown in the dramatic version of the Last Supper, with its hints of El

Greco and the humanity of St. John asleep in front of the preoccupied Christ.

52

53

52. LEANDRO BASSANO (1557–1622)
The Trinity
Copper, $20\frac{1}{4} \times 16\frac{3}{4}$ in (52×43 cm)
Galleria Borghese, Rome

The most prominent of Jacopo da Ponte's sons, Leandro specialized in altarpieces and landscapes. Because of its size and medium this work may have been intended for a chapel in a private house.

53. JACOPO TINTORETTO (1518–94)
St. Mark Liberates a Slave
Oil on canvas, $163\frac{1}{4} \times 213$ in (415×541 cm)
Gallerie dell' Accademia, Venice

This painting has a strangely festive air about it, enhanced by the light background and the great variety of colours. St. Mark was reputed to have been martyred in Alexandria in the reign of the Emperor Nero and in the ninth century his body was brought to Venice, whose patron saint he became to this day.

54

55

54. JACOPO TINTORETTO
Portrait of an Admiral
Oil on canvas, $50 \times 38\frac{3}{4}$ in (127×99 cm)
Uffizi, Florence

This painting is a work of the artist's maturity. Glowing with rich colour and rendering the material of the surcoat with an impressionistic verve, Tintoretto's fine portrait reflects a continuing admiration for his master, Titian.

55. JACOPO TINTORETTO
Leda
Oil on canvas, $63\frac{1}{2} \times 85\frac{3}{4}$ in (162×218 cm)
Uffizi, Florence

Tintoretto treats this recurringly popular theme with a vivacity which owes a good deal to the emphasis he places on the contrasting serpentine lines of the composition – a favourite Mannerist device. The curves of Leda's body form a counterpont with those of the serving maid and with the swan's neck and wings.

56. JACOPO TINTORETTO
Original Sin
Oil on canvas, $59 \times 86\frac{1}{2}$ in (150×220 cm)
Gallerie dell' Accademia, Venice

The luxuriance of the landscape in this painting creates a perfect foil for the sensuous beauty of the two naked bodies. In the background is the subsequent event, the expulsion of the fallen man and woman from Paradise.

56

57

58

57. GIOVANNI BATTISTA MORONI
(*c.*1525–78)
Portrait of a Gentleman
Oil on canvas, 20¾ × 17¾ in (53 × 45 cm)
Pitti, Florence

Acquired for the gallery in 1665 this penetrating study of an old man shows Moroni at his finest. Although Moroni's religious paintings are often criticized for their lack of originality, he is at his best in family portraits.

58. GIOVANNI BATTISTA MORONI
Portrait of Count Pietro Secco-Suardi
Oil on canvas, 72 × 40 in (183 × 102 cm)
Uffizi, Florence

The sombre elegance of the Count pointing at a symbolic flame is emphasized by the sober background in this painting. The picture is relieved, however, by the charming view of a church and house on the left.

59. GIOVANI BATTISTA MORONI
Portrait of a Lady
Oil on canvas, $20\frac{1}{4} \times 17\frac{3}{4}$ in (52×45 cm)
Pitti, Florence

The unfinished background to this portrait enhances its painterly qualities, which seem to anticipate the brushwork *of later artists such as Corot. Moroni's portraits usually have a grey tonality, untypical of Italian work.*

60

60. LUCA CAMBIASO (1527–1585)
Venus and Cupid on the Sea
Oil on canvas, 41½ × 38¾ in (106 × 99 cm)
Galleria Borghese, Rome

A Mannerist who owed much to Venetian painting, *of colour with a taste for rhetorical composition. This is a*
especially to Veronese, Cambiaso combined a delicate sense *particularly decorative and luminous example of his work.*

61. PAOLO VERONESE (1528–1588)
Portrait of Daniele Barbaro
Oil on canvas, 55 × 42 in (140 × 107 cm)
Pitti, Florence

Daniele Barbaro was a man of wide culture and the Venetian ambassador to the court of Elizabeth I of England, which he described in his letters back to the Doge and Senate. In its silvery radiance, this painting shows the influence of the school of Verona where Veronese trained under several minor artists.

62. PAOLO VERONESE
St. John the Baptist Preaching
Oil on canvas, $81\frac{3}{4} \times 55$ in (208×140 cm)
Galleria Borghese, Rome

The frenetic gestures, the varied and complex colours and the emphatic composition of this picture, clearly indicate the influence which Mannerism had on most artists during the late sixteenth century. In Veronese's work, however, Mannerist tendencies are tempered by added Venetian warmth and softness.

63

63. PAOLO VERONESE
The Hommage of Ceres to Venice
Oil on canvas, $121\frac{1}{2} \times 129$ in (309×328 cm)
Gallerie dell' Accademia, Venice

This picture was originally painted for the ceiling of a room in the Doge's Palace, Venice, in which the Magistrato *delle Biade, who controlled everything in Venice to do with corn and grain, had his office.*

64

64. PAOLO VERONESE
The Crucifixion
Oil on canvas, 113 × 176 in (287 × 447 cm)
Gallerie dell' Accademia, Venice

Painted for the church of S. Nicolò della Lattuga ai Frari in Venice, Veronese's conception of the Crucifixion is startlingly novel. Here the major event is crowded into one corner to allow for a wide landscape under a lowering sky.

65. PAOLO VERONESE
The Banquet in the House of Levi
Oil on canvas, 218½ × 504 in (555 × 1280 cm)
Gallerie dell' Accademia, Venice

Despite the religious subject-matter, which landed Veronese in trouble with the Inquisition, this huge painting can best be seen as an idealized version of the magnificence which surrounded the lives of the rich and powerful.

66. PAOLO VERONESE
The Banquet in the House of Levi
Canvas detail
Gallerie dell' Accademia, Venice

The extent to which the artist was able to combine a large-scale picture with a sense of sharply-observed, realistic detail is shown in this detail of four of the figures in the far left of the painting.

65

66

67. GIOVANNI BILIVERT (1576–1644)
The Angel Receives the Gifts of Tobias
Oil on canvas, $68\frac{3}{4} \times 57\frac{1}{4}$ in (175 × 146 cm)
Pitti, Florence

Fantasy, light, colour, a wealth of opulent detail, *who was extremely popular in seventeenth-century*
characterize this work by a painter of Flemish extraction, *Florence. The rendering of the jewellery is superb.*

69

68. FEDERICO BAROCCI (*c.*1528–1612)
The Madonna of the People
Panel, 141¼ × 99 in (359 × 252 cm)
Uffizi, Florence

The cult of the Virgin was greatly fostered by the Jesuits and by all those associated with formulating the tenets of the Counter-Reformation. This crowded composition shows Mary interceding with God for ordinary people.

69. FEDERICO BAROCCI
The Flight of Aeneas from Troy
Oil on canvas, 70¼ × 99½ in (179 × 253 cm)
Galleria Borghese, Rome

The dramatic, theatrical lighting and the emphatic posture of the figures in their painting indicate the extent to which Barocci has absorbed Mannerist conventions. At the same time we can detect that Barocci's sense of realism looks forward to Caravaggio and the Baroque with its powerful chiaroscuro and strong detail.

70

70. ANONYMOUS TUSCAN ARTIST OF THE SIXTEENTH CENTURY
Portrait of Cardinal Marcello Cervini degli
Spannocchi
Panel, $40\frac{1}{2} \times 33\frac{3}{4}$ in (103×86 cm)
Galleria Borghese, Rome

Marcello Cervini was a successful churchman who became a Cardinal in 1539 and later Pope, under the title of Marcello II. He was well-known as a scholar and musician and here the artist has been most successful in catching the air of *interrogative reflection on his face. The carpet detail is reminiscent of those in the portraits of Holbein and Lotto.*

71

71. MICHELANGELO MERISI DA
CARAVAGGIO (1573–1610)
Bacchus
Oil on canvas, $36\frac{1}{2} \times 33\frac{1}{4}$ in (93 × 85 cm)
Uffizi, Florence

Sensuously heavy-lidded, the young Bacchus toys with a glass; a leaf has fallen on the side of the carafe and the fruits are over-ripe. Everything breathes an air of ripeness and self-indulgence typical of Caravaggio's vivid realism.

72. MICHELANGELO MERISI DA CARAVAGGIO
Boy with a Basket of Fruit
Oil on canvas, $27\frac{3}{4} \times 27$ in (71×69 cm)
Galleria Borghese, Rome

The delicate certainty with which Caravaggio has painted the neck and shoulders of the youth who looks languishingly out of this picture, reveals an enormous amount about the artist's personality. The trompe-l'oeil effect of the fruits, *and especially the leaves, with their finely observed traces of decay, as well as the play of light on the cane of the basket, make Caravaggio seem like the progenitor of that 'Magic Realism' which is being practised today.*

73. MICHELANGELO MERISI DA CARAVAGGIO
The Deposition
Oil on canvas, $118 \times 79\frac{3}{4}$ in (300×203 cm)
Musei Vaticani, Rome

Commissioned by Pietro Vittrice for the family chapel in the church of Santa Maria in Vallicella, this picture was painted between 1603 and 1604, when the artist was in his *twenties. It is a complete epitome of the Baroque world, with its dramatic gestures, its strong feeling and sharp sense of immediate reality.*

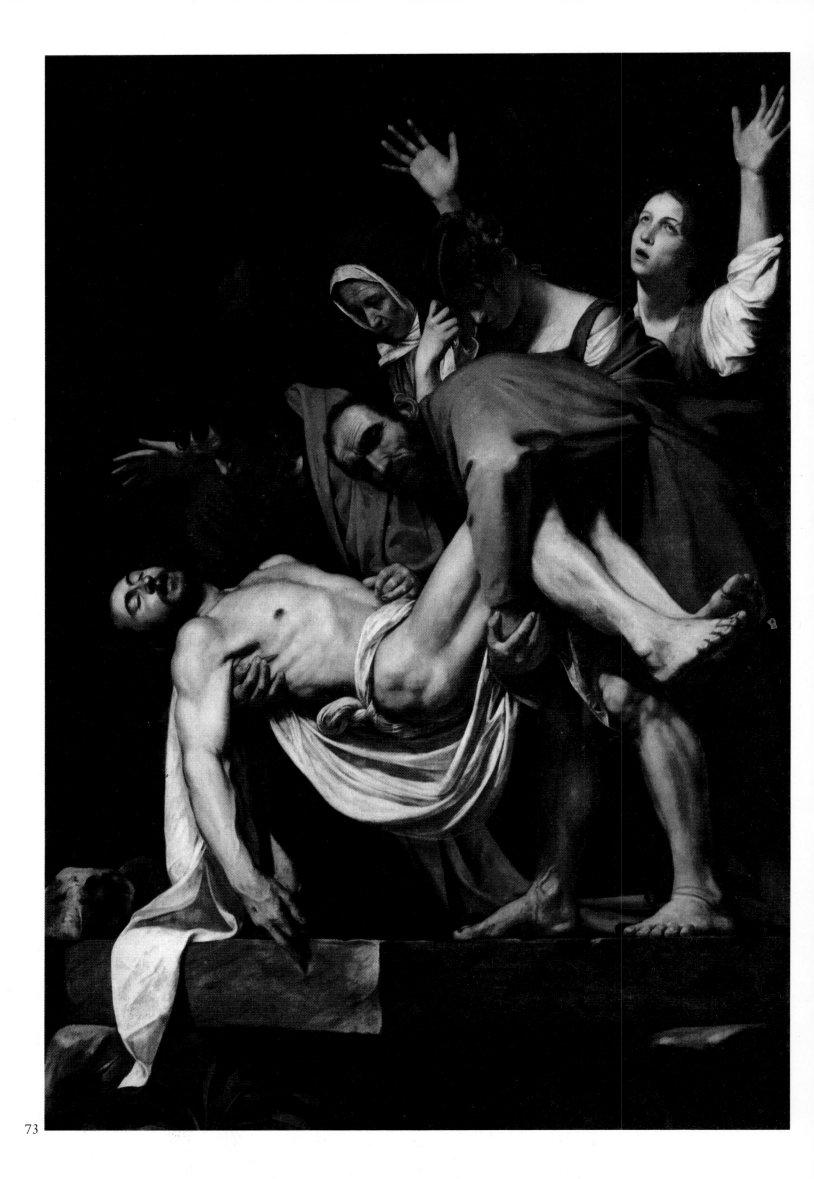

73

74

75

74. RAFFAELLINO DA REGGIO
(1550–78)
Tobias and the Angel
42 × 27 in (107 × 69 cm)
Galleria Borghese, Rome

The heavily accented gestures, the dandyish hair styles and the general feeling of theatricality in this painting typify the advent of the Mannerist attitude which emphasized artificial elegance at the expense of emotional warmth.

75. IPPOLITO SCARSELLA known as
SCARSELLINO (1551-1620)
Christ and his Disciples on the Road to Emmaus
Oil on canvas, $38\frac{1}{2} \times 45\frac{1}{2}$ in (98 × 116 cm)
Galleria Borghese, Rome

United in this one painting are elements from a whole range of pictorial experience. The luminous background and warm colours suggest Titian; the dramatic gestures Mannerism and the studied composition the work of Bolognese artists such as the Carracci brothers and their cousin, Ludovico.

76. SCIPIONE PULZONE (*c.*1550–98)
The Holy Family
Oil on canvas, $53 \times 41\frac{1}{4}$ in (135×105 cm)
Galleria Borghese, Rome

Although superficially there is a debt to Raphael in this painting, this is balanced by a sense of realism. The face of St. Anne, for instance, might have been painted by a *Flemish artist, and there is also emotional realism to be found in the faces of Jesus and John the Baptist, as well as in the down-turned gaze of the Virgin.*

77

77. JACOPO CHIMENTI called
L'EMPOLI (1551–1640)
Still-life
Oil on canvas, 47 × 57 in (120 × 145 cm)
Pitti, Florence

The heightened visual and physical sensibilities of the seventeenth century are reflected in the passion for detailed still-life studies which was to be found in most European countries during that period.

78. ANTIVEDUTO DELLA
GRAMMATICA (1570–1626)
Good Luck
Oil on canvas, 6½ × 53½ in (17 × 136 cm)
Pitti, Florence

A fine example of the new type of genre painting, which was becoming fashionable among the many followers of Caravaggio. *The simple peasant is being cozened by two gypsies, one of whom is rifling his pocket.*

79

79. ANNIBALE CARRACCI (1560–1609)
A Bacchante
Oil on canvas, $43\frac{3}{4} \times 55\frac{3}{4}$ in (112×142 cm)
Uffizi, Florence

Intent on restoring art from its 'decadence', Annibale Carracci went back first to classical prototypes and then to *the great masters of the sixteenth century, to produce art of academic elegance, as typified by this reclining figure.*

80. CRISTOFANO ALLORI (1577–1621)
The Hospitality of St. Julian
Oil on canvas, $102 \times 79\frac{1}{2}$ in (259×202 cm)
Pitti, Florence

This painting hung for many years in the main reception hall of the Grand Dukes in the Pitti and reflects the *influence of Caravaggio imposed on a tradition originating in Florence.*

81

81. FRANCESCO ALBANI (1578–1660)
The Clothing of Venus
Detail of a panel, $60\frac{1}{2}$ in (154 cm) in diameter
Galleria Borghese, Rome

Part of a series of four pictures depicting the history of love, Bacchanalia *with its delightfully luminous grace and this detail might almost be a quotation from Titian's* painterly charm typical of the Venetian master.

82. CRISTOFANO ALLORI (1577–1621)
Judith
Oil on canvas, $54\frac{1}{2} \times 45\frac{1}{2}$ in (139 × 116 cm)
Pitti, Florence

A popular subject in the sixteenth century, the story of Judith contained just those elements of melodrama which appealed to the temper of the age. Judith was an Old Testament heroine who beheaded Holofernes.

83

83. BERNARDO STROZZI (1581–1644)
St. Jerome
Oil on canvas, 22 × 18½ in (56 × 47 cm)
Gallerie dell' Accademia, Venice

There are suggestions in the rich colour and the dramatically conceived lighting of the influence which Rubens was having on Italian art during this period. With Feti, Strozzi kept alive the traditions of Venetian art in the seventeenth century, at a time when the vital centre of Italian art seemed to be moving southwards.

84. MARCANTONIO BASSETTI
(1586–1630)
The Deposition of Christ
Oil on canvas, 18¾ × 14 in (48 × 36 cm)
Galleria Borghese, Rome

Born in Verona, Bassetti was a painter whose work shows the influence of that city's greatest master, Veronese, but mixed with this are to be seen clear signs of the omnipresent dominance of Caravaggio.

84

V

Passion and Ecstasy

IT WAS OBVIOUS that the febrile delights of Mannerism could not be prolonged endlessly and the reactions against the movement came from several different directions. Perhaps the most important was the massing of Catholic forces against Protestantism, which is usually described as the Counter-Reformation. The Council of Trent, which provided the programme and the ideology for the movement, took upon itself the task of purifying the Church from its abuses, tightening up the limits of orthodoxy and providing a new impetus to piety. It was especially concerned with art and music, devoting one session (3 and 4 December 1563) to sacred images, in the course of which it issued the following instructions:

> 'Moreover, let the bishops diligently teach that by means of the stories of the mysteries of our redemption portrayed in paintings and other representations, the people are instructed and confirmed in the articles of faith, also that great profit is derived from all holy images, not only because through the saints the miracles of God and salutory examples are set before the eyes of the faithful, so that they may give God thanks for those things and be moved to adore and love God and cultivate piety. Furthermore, in the invocation of the Saints, the veneration of relics, and the sacred use of images, all superstitions shall be removed, all filthy quest for gain eliminated, and all lasciviousness avoided, so that images shall not be painted and adorned with a seductive charm.'[1]

On the one hand therefore the church had given official sanction to the use of art as a method of instructing the faithful; on the other it had begun to insist that 'lasciviousness' – a quality which much Mannerist painting undoubtedly possessed – should be removed. The first reactions were both ludicrous and lamentable. Pope Paul IV instructed that Michelangelo's nudes in the Sistine Chapel should be covered with curtains, books were published attacking the painter's work and he himself went through a phase of religious conversion. In Venice, on 18 July 1573, Veronese was summoned before the Inquisition and minutely questioned about why he had included secular and vulgar subjects in his religious paintings; they eventually concluded:

> 'that the above-named Paolo would be obliged to improve and change his painting within three months of the day of this admonition, and that according to the opinion and decision of the Holy Tribunal, all the corrections should be made at the expense of the painter, and that if he did not correct the paintings, he would be liable to the penalties imposed by the Holy Tribunal.'[2]

There is no indication that Veronese did retouch his works, or that he suffered any penalties, but in the heart of the Church the ancient statues in the Vatican Palace were dressed in metal skirts and various paintings were touched up to avoid offending the pious.

I

1. MATTIA PRETI (1613–99)
The Healing of the Possessed
Oil on canvas, 53 × 46¼ in (135 × 118 cm)
Uffizi, Florence

Less dramatic than Caravaggio, Preti uses strongly accented lighting, but suffuses the whole canvas with a darkness which owes more to the Venetians than any other school. The importance which artists now attached to drawing and *painting from models is very apparent in the figure of the man possessed by the devil. Preti travelled widely, and his works are to be found in Rome, Naples, Moderna and Malta, where he moved in 1661.*

2. SEBASTIANO MAZZONI
(c.1611–78)
The Annunciation
Oil on canvas, $88\frac{3}{4} \times 61\frac{3}{4}$ in (226×157 cm)
Gallerie dell' Accademia, Venice

From his Florentine upbringing Mazzoni derived a strong sense of perspective and from the Baroque tendencies of his age, a taste for dramatic composition. From the Venetians, amongst whom he spent most of his working life, he also gained a feeling for rich, glowing colour which is *particularly apparent in this vibrant picture. Along with Maffei he preserved the legacy of the Venetian tradition, at a time when the vital movements in Italian art seemed to have passed to Rome and the south, and can be seen as a link with its subsequent revival.*

Oddly enough, even though the decrees of the Council did introduce some sobriety into religious art, in the long run it stimulated other varieties of lasciviousness. This was largely due to the attitudes of the Jesuits, a body of men of great intellectual power and absolute dedication to asserting the primacy of Catholicism, who came to exert a great influence on artistic attitudes. One of the most influential books of the period, *The Spiritual Exercizes* written between 1522 and 1535 by their founder Ignatius of Loyola, sought to exercize a powerful hold over the imagination of its readers by a vivid description of the tortures of hell and the felicities of heaven. This was part of the Jesuit policy – to reach the soul through the senses and emphasize the emotive powers of sensation. Jesuit churches were massive exercises in architectural propaganda, rich with paintings, florid with gold and decoration; the music they favoured was richly emotive; the sermons they preached full of passionate invective, cogent reasoning and evocative metaphors. It was they who contributed so much to making seventeenth-century Baroque art what it was – a sophisticated mechanism for engaging the emotions of the spectator. Agonies and ecstasies were part of its vocabulary, sensationalism its stock-in-trade. The sufferings of saints and martyrs were depicted with frightening realism. St. Sebastian became an especially popular subject, and in countless churches and convents young mens' bodies were shown writhing in tortured passion, arrows clearly embedded in their firm flesh. One Jesuit commentator even went so far as to suggest that in order to depict the sufferings of Christ and the martyrs convincingly, artists should first inflict pain upon themselves.

There was a new awareness of the nature of physical experience which equated the flesh with the spirit, giving both a new equality of significance. A new kind of 'lasciviousness' was born out of this, seen at its most apparent in the most typical monument of the Baroque, Bernini's statue *St. Theresa in Ecstasy*. Here the Saint is all too clearly experiencing an orgasm as the angel thrusts a javelin into her, an accurate account in marble of the Saint's own description of the experience in her autobiography. Bernini was not only a typical artist of the Baroque, but he was also one of the greatest. Patronized by Popes such as Urban VIII, who commissioned from him the great high altar in St. Peter's and the Barberini Palace, and Alexander VII who entrusted him with the design of the colonnade which gave such added splendour to the greatest church in Europe, Bernini was talented in many fields. He was an architect, sculptor, painter (unfortunately, few of his pictures have survived), a wit, a caricaturist and a writer of comedies. His social position was unrivalled and he was constantly in close contact with many of the European sovereigns of his day – Charles I, Louis XIV and Christina of Sweden. He was greatly patronized by the Jesuits, who saw in the dramatic vigour of his works, in their startling realism and in his ability to unite different media – architecture, sculpture, painting, bas-relief into one dramatic whole, a perfect realization of their own aesthetic ideals.

The very concept of realism, which dealt such a death-blow to the idealism of the High Renaissance and the decorative fantasy of Mannerism, seemed to spring up instinctively. One of its first and most brilliant exponents in painting was the Berganese Caravaggio. It was not merely that his technical skills allowed him to portray people and objects with dazzling veracity, but he deliberately avoided any suggestion of

2

3

4

3. MICHELANGELO MERISI
CARAVAGGIO (1573–1610)
Boy with Fruits known as *The Sick Bacchus*
Oil on canvas, 26¼ × 20¾ in (67 × 53 cm)
Galleria Borghese, Rome

It is easy to see from a painting like this, with its startling realism, its unusual pose and lack of idealization, the effect which Caravaggio must have had on his contemporaries, accustomed as they were to more stylized treatment of such subjects. In view of the fact that he died in his thirties Caravaggio's genius – for long neglected – must be seen as one of the most startling phenomena of the time. To him must be attributed a new visual sensibility.

4. MICHELANGELO MERISI
CARAVAGGIO
The Sick Bacchus
Detail of an oil on canvas

This detail expresses in paint something of the quality which marks the poetry of writers such as Herrick, and is indicative of that new sensitivity to the quality of physical experience and the nature of matter.

idealization. His pictures of Bacchus, for instance, look like convincing images of attractive male prostitutes dressed up in a few classical accessories, and he depicts without any scruple ageing flesh, sagging muscles and work-worn skin. Giovanni Pietro Bellori (1615–96), antiquarian, collector and biographer, who was a near contemporary of his wrote disapprovingly:

'He not only ignored the most excellent marvels of the ancients, but actually despised them, and nature alone became the object of his truth. Thus when the most famous statues of Phidias or Glycon were pointed out to him as models for his painting, he had no other reply than to extend his hand to a crowd of men, indicating that nature had provided him sufficiently with teachers.'[3]

5

5. ARTEMISIA GENTILESCHI
(c.1597–1652)
Judith
Oil on canvas, $45\frac{1}{2} \times 36\frac{1}{2}$ in (116×93 cm)
Pitti, Florence

A work which can be dated about 1620, this painting shows the extent to which Biblical stories were endowed at this time with a sense of contemporary reality, shown in the dresses of Judith and her servant. The dramatic intensity is remarkable and enhanced by the fact that the two figures are *looking at something outside the picture space. There is a curious dichotomy between the violence of the scene and a certain clarity, almost simplicity, of presentation. There is a Self-Portrait by Artemisia in the Royal Collection at Hampton Court, near London.*

244

He discovered a new way of seeing: intensely dramatic, precise, which was to have an immense influence on the development of European art as a whole; on artists such as Velazquez, Ribera, Poussin, Vermeer and Rubens. It was the latter who persuaded the Duke of Mantua to buy the *Death of the Virgin* (now in the Louvre in Paris) which had been rejected by the monks who had commissioned it on the grounds that it did not comply with the decrees of the council of Trent, the body of the Virgin having been reputedly modelled on that of a dead prostitute fished out of the Tiber. In his own life Caravaggio presaged that Bohemian image of the artist which became so popular in the nineteenth century. Constantly engaged in brawls and sword fights and suspected of being homosexual, he frequently engaged the attention of the papal police during his stay in Rome. He murdered a man in Rome in 1606 and after this fled to Naples and Sicily; he died at the age of thirty-seven from malaria on his way back to Rome to secure a pardon.

His influence on Italian painters was immediate and powerful. Federico Barocci, for instance, who had been trained in Urbino and practised in a style which was reminiscent of both Raphael and Correggio, took from Caravaggio's work a new concern with lighting effects, which he used with directness and simplicity. Bernardo Cavallino, whose works are tinged with a certain romantic melancholy and who showed something of Titian's sense of warm, vibrant colours, virtually became Caravaggio's artistic heir in Naples. But perhaps the most dedicated disciples of what might legitimately be described as 'Caravaggism' were Orazio Gentileschi and his daughter Artemisia, both of whom worked in London for some time, though Artemisia established herself eventually in Naples which had, by the seventeenth century, become more influential than Florence as an art centre. Her *Judith* has a wild ferocity which goes beyond anything which Caravaggio achieved in visual extravagance; this may be related to the fact that she was raped at the age of fifteen by her art teacher, the painter Agostine Tassi. Another painter who played an important part in the development of art in Naples, and who reflected the combined influences of Caravaggio and Titian was Mattia Preti whose most important work was the decoration of the cathedral of Valletta in Malta. There were, however, those who left Naples, carrying its traditions and innovations elsewhere. Luca Giordano, probably the most prolific artist of the century and known to his contemporaries as *Luca fa presto* or Luca the speed maker, worked first in his native city, then at Monte Cassino, Venice, Florence, Madrid, Toledo and returned to a brilliantly creative old age in Naples. Through his pupil Francesco Solimena, who died in 1747 at the age of ninety, Giordano's influence was carried deep into the heart of the eighteenth century and influenced painters such as Tiepolo and Fragonard.

The sensitivity to realism which Caravaggio had heralded went beyond technical virtuosity, overspilling into the area of subject matter. Increasingly, artists started to portray scenes of contemporary life without attempting to embellish them with any historical or religious significance. This tendency was widespread throughout Europe, and might be seen as not unconnected with the gradual rise to power of merchants and businessmen, the so-called *bourgeoisie*. It reached its height of popularity in Flanders and Holland, and during this period a large number of works from these countries entered the great collections of Italy. The German, Johann Lys, settled in Venice, and Rubens, who lived and worked in Italy for lengthy periods, was patronized by the Popes, the Medici, the Gonzage and the patricians of Genoa. In the hands of an Italian such as Domenico Feti, however, this approach to contemporary life, which had been already hinted at in the works of Annibale Carracci, was marked by an opulent brilliance alien to the colder traditions of Northern art.

Bellori's anecdote about Caravaggio is telling because its author represented another important element in the Baroque; its scholarship, respect for the past and concern with the administrative organization of art itself. The seventeenth century was the age of

Descartes, of Newton, of Galileo, of Spinoza and of Vico; it saw immense strides made in the codification of knowledge and in the development of the natural sciences and this climate affected art itself. An early result of this was the establishing of academies for the training of artists. One of the first of these had been started by the sculptor Baccio Bandinelli (1493–1560) who had been commissioned by Pope Leo X to make a copy of the *Laocoön* in the Belvedere Gardens, and used one of the rooms in the Vatican which had been allotted to him for meeting young artists to whom he taught the rudiments of anatomy and life-drawing. He also commissioned the engraver Agostino Veneziano to produce instructional diagrams of human figures so that they could be copied by students. In 1562 Duke Cosimo de' Medici set up an Academy of Drawing in Florence, with himself and Michelangelo as the joint heads; thirty-six artist members were elected and provision was also made for amateurs and connoisseurs. But it was in Bologna, under the aegis of the Carracci family that the concept of the academy was translated into an attitude to art. The *Accademia degli Incammati* (Academy of Beginners) which they founded reflected a scholarly concern with painting which was to have a profound influence on the history of European art. In the development of these teaching processes and all that they implied, the dominant figure was Agostino Carracci whose systematic anatomical studies were published as engravings in book form, and dominated art school teaching for some two centuries. A collector, a scholar and a painter of uneven talents, he joined his brother Annibale who was working in Rome on the decoration of the Farnese Gallery, which was to be seen throughout the seventeenth and eighteenth centuries as the peer of Michelangelo's Sistine Chapel ceiling and Raphael's decorations for the Vatican. The Farnese decorations became a repertory of images, gestures and compositional devices on which countless artists were to draw. They were a remarkable exercize in meticulously planned decoration; Annibale made thousands of preparatory drawings, an indication of the new more intellectualized attitude to creativity. Annibale was, however, artistically versatile. He was one of the earliest practitioners of the new art form of caricature and he produced some of the first examples of pure genre painting – recording impressions of contemporary life, such as the inside of a butcher's shop, groups of peasants eating – scenes which Caravaggio might have introduced into large paintings as incidentals.

The impact which the Carracci had on Bologna made that city almost as important in the history of eighteenth-century painting as Rome, to which many of its painters eventually made their way, especially during the reign of the Bolognese Pope Gregory XV. One of their most exceptional pupils was Guido Reni who, though he is generally known for his extremely popular religious paintings still to be seen in Roman Catholic homes in great numbers, is a far more significant artist than these would suggest. The kind of classical training he had received in Bologna steeled him against too facile a dependence on Caravaggio, and he retained in his work something of those Hellenistic tendencies which had marked the High Renaissance. His influence on his fellow Bolognese, Gian-Francesco Barbieri known, because of his squint, as Guercino, was significant and did something to dilute the lively sensuality which marked that artist's earlier works. If Reni's work cast side glances back at the Renaissance, his successor as the leading painter of Bologna, Giuseppe Maria Crespi, produced works with something of the Surrealist quality which had marked the works of the Mannerists – using vivid realism to depict either genre scenes or historical subjects of a violent character.

6. JAN LYS (1500–1629)
Apollo and Marsyas
Oil on canvas, $22\frac{3}{4} \times 18\frac{3}{4}$ in (58 × 48 cm)
Gallerie dell' Accademia, Venice

There is an oratorical vehemence about this picture which suggests the dramatic preoccupations of the generation of the early Baroque. The colouring has the soft effulgence of the Venetian tradition and the composition the drama of Roman art. Lys typified the close connexions which existed at this time between Italy and the Low Countries. Born in Germany and trained in Holland, he arrived in Rome at the age of twenty-two and spent the rest of his life there, dying eventually in Venice. He was mainly responsible for bringing the influence of Caravaggio to the North.

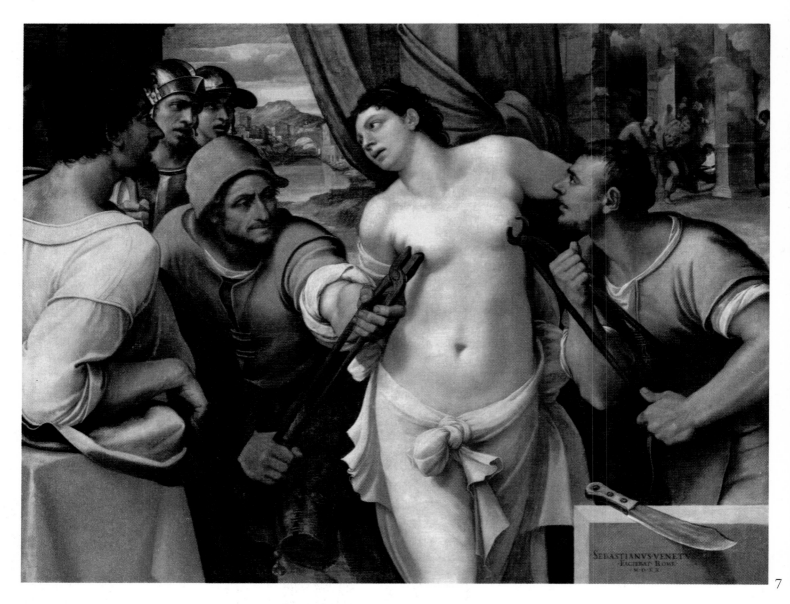

7. SEBASTIANO DEL PIOMBO
(1485–1547)
The Martyrdom of St. Agatha
Panel, 50 × 66¾ in (127 × 170 cm)
Pitti, Florence

This painting formed part of the Urbino collection and enjoyed a great success when it was painted in 1520, possibly because of the sadistic appeal hidden beneath its hagiographic detail. Although Piombo had studied under Giovanni Bellini, the most important influence on him had been Giorgione. He moved from Venice to Rome in 1511 where he was involved in painting the Villa Farnese, and was given a post in the papal Mint – hence his cognomen. He became a friend of Michelangelo, who secured commissions for him and influenced his style.

8. LELIO ORSI (1511–87)
St. Cecilia and Valerian
Oil on canvas, 30½ × 23½ in (78 × 60 cm)
Galleria Borghese, Rome

At once naive and mannered, spontaneous and theatrically contrived, this charming work contains elements which a later generation would see as verging on Surrealism. There is a strong element of eclecticism in Orsi's work – the lighting effects in this painting clearly owe a debt to Correggio and the contrived pose of the figures are a reflection of Parmigianino's compositional devices. The whole composition of the painting suggests the theatre.

9. MARCO PINA DA SIENA (1525–88)
The Ascension
Panel, 51½ × 39¾ in (131 × 101 cm)
Galleria Borghese, Rome

Painted for the church of S. Lucia del Gonfalone in Rome, this epitome of Baroque religious painting shows the pictorial sensibilities of the Sienese tradition wedded to the legacy of Raphael and Michelangelo. This is especially apparent in the muscularity of the naked figures, the postures of their bodies and the declamatory gestures of the soldiers, some of which seem to have been based on the figures in the Sistine Chapel ceiling. The compositional pattern with its diagonals framing the figure of the risen Christ, is extremely effective.

8

9

11

10. PELLEGRINO TIBALDI (1527–96)
The Adoration of the Child Jesus
Oil on canvas, $61\frac{3}{4} \times 41\frac{1}{4}$ in (157×105 cm)
Galleria Borghese, Rome

Signed and dated 1549, this is a remarkable work for a young man of twenty-two. The influence of the nudes on the Sistine Chapel ceiling is apparent, but it has been digested into the creation of a massively imposing conception. Tibaldi after doing some work in Bologna on his return from Rome in 1553, turned from painting to architecture, and carried out important work in the Duomo at Milan. This was so successful that he was summoned to Madrid by Philip II in 1585 to supervise the building of the Escorial and to carry out sculpture and paintings for its decoration.

11. ORAZIO GENTILESCHI (1565–1639)
Judith with the Head of Holofernes
Oil on canvas, $57\frac{1}{4} \times 103\frac{1}{2}$ in (146×263 cm)
Musei Vaticani, Rome

Born in Pisa and brought up in the Florentine tradition, Gentileschi moved to Rome and there experienced the impact of Caravaggio. The result was works of startling clarity and realism. His daughter, Artemisia, also painted the same subject. Gentileschi was one of the first main international figures in the art world of his time, leaving Genoa for Paris in 1625 where he worked for Marie de' Medici. He was then called to London by Charles I, where he carried out extensive work at Hampton Court and at the Queen's House in Greenwich. He was highly thought of in England and as one of the first practitioners of Caravaggism had an important influence on the native school of painting.

12. GIOVANNI BATTISTA CARACCIOLO called IL BATTISTELLO (c. 1570–1630)
Salome
Oil on canvas, $48\frac{1}{4} \times 58$ in (123×148 cm)
Uffizi, Florence

A typical representative of the Neapolitan school, this artist was brought up under the shadow of Caravaggio, whose influence is clear in the realism of the figures and in the dramatic lighting. Battistello still retained, however, a liking for the curvilinear compositional syntax of Manner-ism. The strong accents of realism in this painting have an almost Flemish intensity about them, and the play of light on the faces of Salome and the old woman are important elements in its compositional structure. In his later works Battistello's style became less emphatic.

13. GUIDO RENI (1575–1642)
Moses with the Tablets of the Law
Oil on canvas, $68\frac{1}{2} \times 52\frac{1}{2}$ in (174×134 cm)
Galleria Borghese, Rome

Resisting the influence of Caravaggio and tending to revert to the Raphaelesque classicism of the High Renaissance, Guido brought to painting such as this a gift of lucid composition and a feeling for broad, emphatically accented colours. His superb mastery of lighting effects and the sensuality of his fluent line were qualities which recom-mended him to his contemporaries, though they also explain the disfavour with which he was regarded by nineteenth-century critics such as John Ruskin who felt such characteristics were facile and lacking in moral strength.

13

14. GUIDO RENI
Bacchus as a Child
Oil on canvas, $34 \times 27\frac{1}{2}$ in (87×70 cm)
Pitti, Florence

A work of the period between 1616–20, this highly decorative painting with its wealth of detailed observation and its slight sense of idealization, makes an interesting contrast with Caravaggio's treatment of similar subjects.

The light tones and transparent flesh tints which are apparent in a work such as this reveal the delicate mastery of execution which redeems even the most sentimental of his many works.

15

15. MATTEO ROSSELLI (1578–1651)
The Triumph of David
Oil on canvas, $79\frac{3}{4} \times 79\frac{3}{4}$ in (203 × 203 cm)
Pitti, Florence

Cardinal Carlo de' Medici commissioned this work from the painter in 1621 and a replica (now in the Louvre) was made in 1630. It was the artist's most successful painting, replete with a sense of triumphal joy, forward movement *and sparkling vitality. The painter's handling of textures is especially noteworthy in the way he has contrasted the different materials worn by the girls on either side of the young David.*

16

16. FRANCESCO ALBANI (1578–1660)
The Triumph of Diana
Oil on canvas, 60½ in (154 cm) in diameter
Galleria Borghese, Rome

Part of a series of The History of Love *bought by Cardinal Scipione Borghese in 1622, Albani's work reflects the influence of Domenichino, but it is also an important example of the way in which Bolognese painting was developing after the Carracci. Albani actually co-operated*

with Annibale Carracci in the decoration of the Farnese Palace, but returned to his native Bologna in 1616, where he continued to produce idyllic landscapes and allegorical paintings. These became very popular in the eighteenth century, especially amongst English collectors.

17

17. ORAZIO RIMINALDI (1586–1631)
Love the Artificer or *Love the Conqueror*
Oil on canvas, $55\frac{1}{2} \times 43\frac{3}{4}$ in (141 × 112 cm)
Pitti, Florence

Showing the influence of Caravaggio, but with a greater emphasis on draughtsmanship, this work was acquired for the Pitti in the 1620s by Prince Ferdinando, the son of Cosimo II. The artist is known mainly for his frescoes in the cathedral of Pisa. There is an apparent debt to Hellenistic sculpture in the pose of the figure in this picture, though this has been partly weakened by the realism of the face which seems that of a tired street boy.

19

20

18. DOMENICO FETI (1589–1624)
The Parable of the Vineyard or *The Workers in
the Vineyard*
Panel, $29\frac{1}{2} \times 17\frac{1}{4}$ in (75 × 44 cm)
Pitti, Florence

*Commissioned by Cardinal Leopoldo de' Medici in 1675,
this painting was stolen by the Nazis during the last war
and retrieved in 1955. It is one of a series illustrating
parables from the New Testament and exemplifies Feti's
magnificent sense of decorative scale. From 1613 until 1622
he was court painter to Mantua and many of his works are
now in England in the Royal collection, having been
purchased with the bulk of that collection in 1628.*

19. DOMENICO FETI
The Lost Drachma
Panel, $29\frac{1}{2} \times 17\frac{1}{4}$ in (75 × 44 cm)
Pitti, Florence

*Feti's liking for the kind of composition which leaves a large
amount of space in the upper parts of the picture is strikingly
demonstrated in this work where the theatrical lighting adds
another element of interest. It might almost be a scene from a
popular comedy. There are obvious parallels between a
work such as this and that of the Le Nain brothers.*

21

20. GIOVAN FRANCESCO BARBIERI
known as GUERCINO (1591–1666)
Apollo and Marsyas
Oil on canvas, 73 × 80½ in (186 × 205 cm)
Pitti, Florence

Painted for the Grand Duke Cosimo II in 1618 and huge in scale, this work shows the extent to which Barbieri combined a luminous sense of colour with a monumentality of conception which echoes Michelangelo. It reveals too the debt which he owes to Ludovico Carracci. Much of his early work was done in Bologna where he was patronized by the Archbishop, with whom he moved to Rome in 1621 when that prelate was elected Pope with the title of Gregory XV.

21. GIOVANNI MANNOZZI (1592–1636)
The Parish Priest Arlotto
Oil on canvas, 45½ × 36 in (116 × 92 cm)
Pitti, Florence

A famous Florentine figure of the fifteenth century, whose witticisms became part of folk-lore, Father Arlotto is portrayed by Mannozzi in a straightforward portrait – obviously based on a model. The rendering of the face is especially fine. The lighting is curiously capricious and seems to be coming from different sources. A good deal of the effectiveness of the composition stems from the bizarre shape of the padre's hat.

22. PIETRO BERRETTINI DA CORTONA (1596–1669)
Ceiling detail of the Sala di Marte in the Pitti, Florence

After studying at Rome, paying special attention to the decorative schemes of Raphael and achieving enormous fame for his painting in the Barberini Palace, Pietro went to Florence to carry out a series of decorations in the Pitti Palace for Ferdinand II, Grand Duke of Tuscany, of which this is one. Cortona was also an architect of distinction and this is apparent from the quality of his paintings which are often, as in this case, specially designed for their architectural effects. His illusionistic skill allowed him to become one of the most brilliant exponents of that technique known as di sotto in sù, the figures being painted in such a way that they seem to be suspended in space.

22

23. PIETRO BERRETTINI DA CORTONA
Portrait of Marcello Saccheti
Oil on canvas, $59\frac{3}{4} \times 53\frac{3}{4}$ in (152×137 cm)
Galleria Borghese, Rome

The influence of *Van Dyck* is clearly apparent in this effortlessly elegant portrait, with the highlights appearing on the hands, the face and the ruff. There is a pleasing severity about the whole composition which contrasts with the more spectacular portraits of some of his contemporaries.

Pietro da Cortona was very conscious of the spirit of his age and in 1652, in collaboration with another artist, he published a Treatise on Painting which enshrined the ideals of the Council of Trent about the role of art in contemporary morality and society.

24

24. GIAN LORENZO BERNINI (1598–1680)
Portrait of a Boy
Oil on canvas, 14 × 11¾ in (36 × 30 cm)
Galleria Borghese, Rome

An architect and sculptor, Bernini confined his exercises in portraiture to self-portraits and paintings of his friends and relations. It has been suggested that this charming and intimate picture is a portrait of his younger brother. Bernini clearly saw himself as a universal man, in the pattern of Leonardo, and it would seem that he frequently used paintings for his portrait busts. The triple portrait head of Charles I by Van Dyck, for example, was carried out as a model upon which he could base his sculpture of the King – subsequently destroyed in a fire at Whitehall.

265

25

25. GIAN LORENZO BERNINI
David
Detail of a marble statue, 66¾ in (170 cm)
Galleria Borghese, Rome

The look of determination and concentration on the face of the young David as he aims his sling at Goliath is indicative of the detail which Bernini put into his works. The sensitivity of the interpretation is an indication of those qualities which brought the artist such fame as a portrait sculptor, combining realism with grace and emotion.

26. GIAN LORENZO BERNINI
Aeneas, Anchises and Ascanius
Marble, 86½ in (220 cm)
Galleria Borghese, Rome

This statue of Aeneas carrying his father from Troy and accompanied by the young Ascanius, shows the beginning of Bernini's preoccupation with movement around a vertical axis. It has been suggested that part of the work may have been carried out by his father, Pietro Bernini. This was one of the works he carried out for Cardinal Scipione Borghese when he was in his early twenties. It shows the remarkable precocity of his technical gifts and the extent to which he had broken away, even at this stage, from the tradition of Mannerism.

27. GIAN LORENZO BERNINI
The Rape of Proserpine
Marble, 88½ in (225 cm)
Galleria Borghese, Rome

Bernini produced this work between 1621 and 1622 and it shows his sculptural style in its perfection. The penetration of space is emphasized by the differing angles of projection; there is a sense of movement and drama and, of course, meticulous workmanship. The concern with rotation persisted throughout Bernini's artistic career.

26

27

28

28. ANDREA SACCHI (1559–1661)
Portrait of Monsignor Clemente Merlini
Oil on canvas, $59 \times 53\frac{3}{4}$ in (150×137 cm)
Galleria Borghese, Rome

This portrait of a leading member of the papal bureaucracy, an Auditor of the Sacred Rota, shows us a man of wit, warmth and intelligence. The style shows a combination of Italian realism with that type of elegance which Van Dyck was popularizing in the courts of Europe. An enthusiastic supporter of the classical tradition of Raphael against what *he saw as the excesses of the Baroque, Sacchi was at his most individual in his portraits. It was this aspect of his output which is apparent in the work of his pupils such as Carlo Maratta. Many of his religious works are in St. Peter's, and he was responsible for the redecoration of the Lateran Baptistry in Rome.*

29

30

31

29. FRANCESCO MAFFEI (c.1600–60)
Perseus with the Head of Medusa
Oil on canvas, 51×63¼ in (130×161 cm)
Gallerie dell' Accademia, Venice

An artist whose reputation was only re-established in the 1950s, Maffei had a passion for turbulent scenes, rich colours and complex compositions. It has been said that his style with its bizarre fantasy and opulent tonalities links El Greco and Gaudi, but more obviously his work is linked with that of the great Venetians such as Tintoretto. A native of Verona, most of his work was carried out in the northern part of the Venetian Republic.

30. FRANCESCO FURINI (1603–46)
Hylas and the Nymphs
Oil on canvas, 90½×102½ in (230×261 cm)
Pitti, Florence

Painted for Agnolo Galli c1638, this large work is notable for the sensuality of the figures of the nymphs and the sense of movement brought into relief by the heavy, brooding sky. It is in paintings of this kind that one may already detect elements of a proto-romanticism, which was to smoulder away beneath the façade of much seventeenth-century art.

31. PIER FRANCESCO MOLA (1612–66)
St. Peter Liberated from Prison
Oil on canvas, 76½×56½ in (195×144 cm)
Galleria Borghese, Rome

Nurtured in the traditions of northern Italy, Mola came to Rome in 1650 and exercized an important influence on the development of the late Baroque style there. This particular work seems designed to show his skill in manipulating perspective, an exercise slightly devalued by the fact that the angel seems to be resting on a mattress made of cloud. In his early life Mola had been in close contact with both Guido Beni and Guercino, the influence of both painters being apparent in much of his work, but he also had a very Venetian feeling for warm, glowing colours.

32. SALVATOR ROSA (1615–73)
Scene Near a Port
Detail of an oil on canvas, 91½×157 in
(233×399 cm) Pitti, Florence

Painted when the artist was living in Florence between 1640 and 1649, the painting, of which this is a detail, was brought by Cardinal Gian Carlo de' Medici. The new sense of sharp social observation which was becoming fashionable is apparent in this charming bathing scene. There are apparent affinities with classical painting at Pompeii.

33. SALVATOR ROSA
The Broken Bridge
Oil on canvas, $41\frac{1}{2} \times 50$ in (106×127 cm)
Pitti, Florence

It is easy to see why eighteenth-century connoisseurs with their romantic sensibilities should have been so attracted by Salvator Rosa's images of decaying buildings in wild, untamed landscapes. His later attempts to rival the religious and allegorical works of his Roman contemporaries resulted in rather pretentious and empty works, lacking entirely the freshness of vision of paintings like this. The painter's taste for ruins and his skill in depicting them can be seen in the stone-work of the bridge, surmounted by the Medici arms. The rugged hill-side is observed with the same love.

34. BERNARDO CAVALLINO
(1616–54)
Esther and Asheurus
Oil on canvas, $29\frac{1}{2} \times 40$ in (75 × 102 cm)
Uffizi, Florence

Succeeding Caravaggio as the most popular painter of seventeenth-century Naples, Cavallino owed his reputation to a stylistic elegance which seems to reflect the influence of Van Dyck, and to his ability to create *compositions which have an immediately obvious sense of balance about them. Part of the quality of his work stems from the fact that he painted over a deep red bole background which gives a fresco-like effect.*

35

35. CARLO DOLCI (1616–86)
Portrait of Fra Arnolfi de' Bardi, Knight of Jerusalem
Oil on canvas, $58\frac{1}{2} \times 46\frac{3}{4}$ in (149 × 119 cm)
Pitti, Florence

This portrait of a member of a leading Florentine family was bequeathed to the gallery in 1954 by Count Bardi Serzelli, one of his descendants. Although Arnolfi is wearing the cloak of his order, he is dressed in a Hungarian-style uniform. Dolci was a native of Florence and spent his whole working life in that city with most of his commissions coming from its richer citizens. His portraits are generally preferable to his more elaborate historical or religious paintings, which are marred by a certain unctuousness of manner.

36. CARLO MARATTA (1625–1713)
Portrait of Clement IX
Oil on canvas, 57 × 46¼ in (145 × 118 cm)
Musei Vaticani, Rome

This commanding portrait of a pope who only reigned for two years between 1677 and 1679 might almost pass as a Velasquez in terms of its penetrating analysis of personality, its richness of colour and the convincing depiction of textiles and the physical quality of matter. In feeling Maratta was closer to the classical traditions of Raphael than he was to the more dramatic tendencies of the Baroque and his influence was wider than might have been expected, largely due to the fact that he maintained a large workshop, where numerous pupils absorbed his style.

37. LUCA GIORDANO (1631–1705)
The Crucifixion of St. Peter
Oil on canvas, 77 × 101½ in (196 × 258 cm)
Gallerie dell' Accademia, Venice

The Neapolitan Luca Giordano worked for the Medici in Florence during the 1680s and it is to this period that this work must be attributed. In his command of dazzling perspective and bright luminous colour he anticipated the great decorative artists of the eighteenth century. His style has a superb self-confidence, and his output was prodigious, much of it to be seen in Spain where he worked for Charles II for ten years in Madrid, Toledo and the Escorial. His work combines brilliantly the Neapolitan and Venetian artistic traditions.

38. FRANCESCO SOLIMENA (1657–1743)
Rebecca and Jacob at the Well
Oil on canvas, 79½ × 59 in (202 × 150 cm)
Gallerie dell' Accademia, Venice

In the magnificence of this composition, with its melodramatic background, its ingenious arrangement of the figures and eloquence of gesture, there is some indication of how Solimena's work prepares the ground for Piazetta.

37

38

VI

The Kingdom of the Senses

THE INTELLECTUALIZATION OF art, which had been proceeding apace since the beginning of the sixteenth century, had other results emphasized not only by the growth of academies, the artistic disciplines of the Bolognese School and the improving social status of the artist, but by the emergence of connoisseurs such as Bellori. The most important result was the growing importance attached to art collections as significant factors in the evolution of taste and style. Collecting works of art as opposed to commissioning them for a specific purpose had, of course, always happened, but by the seventeenth century it had assumed a new professionalism of approach, a more deliberate attitude of conspicuous expenditure, promoting scholarship and encouraging closer study of the art of the past.

Here again the Medici were in the forefront. The elder branch of the family had died out in 1537, and Cosimo, whose mother had been a granddaughter of Lorenzo the Magnificent, became first Duke and then Grand Duke of Tuscany. He was a man of immense wealth, having married Eleanora of Toledo. With the assistance of Bronzino and the connoisseur, painter, architect and historian Giorgio Vasari (1511–74) he set about making the Medici collection the most important in Europe. He gathered together again many of the family treasures which had been dispersed in 1494 and 1527 when the Medici had been deposed from power. He paid for important archaeological excavations to be carried out at Chiusi and Arezzo, the results of which were the discovery of traces of Etruscan civilization. The fruits of these efforts are the basis of the Etruscan Museum at Chiusi which today is one of the finest of its kind. In 1549 he had acquired the Pitti Palace, the bridge of which had been started in 1440 by Luca Pitti, one of the great rivals of the Medici, which has been left unfinished. Bartolommeo Ammanati (1511–92) was commissioned to complete it, and it became the Duke's official residence, beautified still further by the Bobboli Gardens behind it. Eleven years later Cosimo entrusted Vasari with the design of another building, the Uffizi, on the other bank of the Arno, near the Palazzo Vecchio, the two palaces being connected with a covered passage over the Ponte Vecchio, which now contains the famous collection of self-portraits which had been started by Duke Cosimo III (1642–1723).

Duke Francis I (1547–1608), the son of Cosimo and Eleanora, started to organize the Uffizi, which Cosimo had used as offices and workshops for craftsmen who were furnishing his palaces, into a gallery more sophisticated than the old *guardaroba* which had housed most of the paintings and statues. He was succeeded by his brother, the fiery Ferdinand, who until then had been a cardinal, living in Rome, building the lovely Villa Medici on the Pincio (now the French Academy in Rome) and collecting a magnificent group of Greek and Roman statues which he brought back to Florence with him. He commissioned the appropriately named Bernardo Buontalenti (1536–1608), architect, military engineer, painter, sculptor and firework expert, to

I

1. FRANCESCO GUARDI (1712–93)
The Island of S. Giorgio
Oil on canvas, $28\frac{1}{2} \times 38$ in $(72 \times 97$ cm$)$
Gallerie dell' Accademia, Venice

Reminiscent almost of the works of Turner in his handling of paint and his concern with effects of light and atmosphere, *Guardi was a painter who was especially adept at depicting the soft radiance of the Venetian lagoons.*

2

2. GIAN LORENZO BERNINI (1598–1680)
Bust of Cardinal Scipione Borghese
Marble, 30½ in (78 cm) high
Galleria Borghese, Rome

It is appropriate that Cardinal Scipione Borghese, the founder of the gallery which bears his name, should have been portrayed by one of the many artists – Caravaggio is *another – who owed so much to him. It was executed a year before the Cardinal's death in 1632. One of history's great connoisseur's, Scipione became an early patron of Bernini.*

construct additional rooms, including the well-known Tribuna. But it was during the fifty-year-old reign of Duke Ferdinand II (1608–70) that all these earlier efforts came to full fruition. He himself was not only an enthusiastic and judicious collector, but through his wife, Vittoria delle Rovere, had inherited the artistic treasures of the Dukes of Urbino. With his two brothers, the Cardinals Giovanni Carlo (1611–27) and Leopoldo (1616–75), these men of immense intellectual curiosity and learning gave the whole of their own large, personal collections to the family treasure house; those of Giovanni Carlo went into the Pitti, those of Leopoldo into the Uffizi. These two galleries created a pattern upon which all the princely galleries of Europe, used at this time to enhance the prestige of their owners, as well as to delight the eyes of visitors, were modelled. Cosimo III, Ferdinand's rather unpleasant successor, added the collection of Dutch and Flemish works.

In some ways the most remarkable of the Medici was a woman, and one whose name has little fame. Florence had for long been an object of envy to the great powers, and in October 1735 England, France, Austria and Holland agreed that as part of a general peace the Grand Duchy should be given to Maria Theresa, in exchange for her husband's Duchy of Lorraine, which went to France. The only surviving Medici was Anna Maria Ludovica (1674–1743), the daughter of Cosimo III, who was the widow of the Elector Palatine. Trained as a collector by her great-uncle, Cardinal Leopoldo, she had significantly increased the Medici collections, and in her will she gave 'to the State of Tuscany' forever all the Medici collections in Florence, Rome and elsewhere on condition, 'that none of these collections should ever be removed from Florence, and that they should be for the benefit of the public of all nations'. Only Napoleon and Hitler have subsequently tried to interfere with that remarkable provision, which has established the Medici as the first public benefactors of European culture.

Theirs was the most magnificent example, but it was not the only instance of the new attitude to collecting. All over Europe great and small collections were being built up – those of Thomas Howard, Earl of Arundel, and the Stuarts in England (the first public museum, the Ashmolean, was opened in England in the 1670s), of the Hapsburgs in Vienna, of the Kings of Spain in the Escorial. There were smaller collections too of considerable importance. In Rome Cardinal Scipione Borghese (1576–1633) a nephew of Paul V, and one of Bernini's most active patrons, commissioned the Dutch architect Vansanzio to build on the Pincio a villa designed partly as a residence, but predominantly as a museum, to house his own superb collection. A connoisseur of eclectic tastes, who had a special admiration for the great Venetians, he disposed his collection throughout the palace on the same plan which is observed today. It is not without interest to read how the villa appeared to John Evelyn, himself an example of the new type of virtuoso, when he visited it on 7 November, 1644:

'I walked to the Villa Borghese, a house and ample garden on Mons Pincius, yet somewhat without the City walls, circumscribed by another wall full of small turrets and banqueting houses, which makes it appear at a distance like a little towne. Within it is an Elysium of delight, having in the centre a noble Palace; but the entrance of the garden presents us with a very glorious fabrick or rather dorecase, adorned with excellent marble statues . . . . The house is square with turrets from which the prospect is excellent towards Rome and the invironing hills, covered as they now are with snow, which indeed commonly continues a great part of the summer, affording great refreshment. Round the house is a balustre of white marble, with frequent jetts of water, and adorned with a multitude of statues. The walls of the house are covered with antiq incrustations of history, as that of Curtius, the Rape of Europa, Leda &c. The cornices above consist of fruitages and festoons, between which are niches furnished with statues, which order is to be seen everywhere, even to the roofs. In the lodge at the entry are divers good statues of consuls &c. with two pieces of field artillery (a mode much practized in Italy before the great mens' houses) which they look on as a piece of state rather than a defence. In the first hall within are the 12 Roman Emperors, of excellent marble; 'twixt them stand porphry columns and other precious stones of vast height and magnitude, with urnes of Oriental alabaster, tables of *Pietra-Commessa*. Here is that renowned Diana which Pompey worshipped; the most incomparable Seneca, of touch bleeding in a huge vase of porphyric, resembling the dropps of his blood; the so famous gladiator, and the Hermaphrodite upon a quilt of stone. The new piece of Daphne, and David of Cavaliero Bernini is observable for the pure whiteness of the stone, and the art of the statuary, which is stupendious. There are a multitude of rare pictures of infinite value by the best masters; huge tables of porphyrie, and two exquisitely wrought vases of the same. In another chamber are divers instruments of musiq. . . . The perspective is considerable, composed by the position of looking glasses, which render a strange multiplication of things resembling divers most richly furnished roomes. Here stands a rare clock of German worke; in a worde, nothing but what is magnificent is to be seen.'[1]

3

The Villa Borghese today is still almost exactly the same as it was then.

Paradises such as this were becoming more common as the seventeenth century moved into the eighteenth. Something of the intellectual rigours of the Renaissance, and the religious fervours of the Baroque was being abated, in a new world of private luxury and public elegance. Charles II was not the only monarch to give hedonism a social cachet and art began to reflect a feeling of voluptuous self-indulgence. Portraiture became increasingly popular in a world which paid much attention to projecting the image of the individual. The elegant young aristocrats who peer down from the paintings of Carlo Dolci, the moustachioed gallants of Pietro da Cortona and the astute churchmen of Andrea Sacchi or Carlo Maratta represent a world concerned less with the ecstacies of the soul than with those of the body. There was a new feeling too for landscape as a subject suitable in itself for the attention of the artist. In the 1640s one of the favoured *proteges* of the Medici was Salvator Rosa, who in 1635, at the age of twenty, had left his native Naples to make a name for himself as painter, poet, actor, satirist and musician, but had been forced to move to Florence to escape the hostility of the all-powerful Bernini whom he had satirized in his drawings. Trained originally as a battle-painter, he evolved a remarkable style, which had a great deal to do with the evolution of the concept of the Picturesque, especially in England, and which gives him some standing as one of the precursors of Surrealism. Endowed with a restless and febrile imagination and a wild, romantic vision, he painted landscapes which verged on the fantastic in their *farouche* exuberance and which were often peopled with alarming or unlikely characters.

Men such as John Evelyn typified the attitude of respectful admiration with which the rest of Europe had come to regard Italy by the beginning of the eighteenth century and the Grand Tour, which was concerned mainly with that country, was not confined to the English. Many painters such as Rosalba Carriera with her delicate style, her ability to create an impression of innocent veracity, achieved spectacular success

3. CARLO DOLCI (1616–86)
A Young Man of the Bardi Family
Oil on canvas, 22¾ × 18 in (58 × 46 cm)
Pitti, Florence

According to an inscription on the canvas, this portrait was painted by Dolci when he was fifteen. If this is true his precocity is remarkable. The painting of the rich embroidery of the clothes is as impressive as the observation of the face.

4. GIOVANNO ANTONIO PELLEGRINI (1675–1741)
Allegory of Sculpture
Oil on canvas, 56¼ × 51¾ in (143 × 132 cm)
Gallerie dell' Accademia, Venice

A work of the artist's later period, this painting is noteworthy for the fine handling of surfaces – not only of the dress, but also of the stonework behind. There is a fine sculptural quality too in the painting of the figure.

4

5. GIOVANNI BATTISTA TIEPOLO
(1696–1770)
The Transfer of the Holy House to Loreto
Oil on canvas, $48\frac{3}{4} \times 33\frac{1}{4}$ in (124×85 cm)
Gallerie dell' Accademia, Venice

This improbable subject – the house in which Jesus lived at Nazareth being transported through the sky for some unlikely reason to the town of Loreto in Italy – has given scope to the artist for one of his most splendid works. The painting is all light, movement and luminous magnificence, tricked out with remarkable effects of perspective.

throughout Europe, and was showered with commissions by visiting foreigners. Her brother-in-law, Giovanni Antonio Pellegrini, who had become especially adept at producing exercizes in that splendid, decorative style which flourished in Venice during the eighteenth century, worked in Düsseldorf, Mannheim, Paris and Vienna before arriving in England in 1708 in the train of the English ambassador to Venice, the Earl of Manchester. He carried out important works at Kimbolton Castle, Castle Howard and Narford House, Norfolk and had a decisive influence on English decorative idioms. His successor Jacopo Amigoni followed a similar international circuit. Born in Naples he worked in Venice, moved on to Bavaria, where he decorated the castles of Nymphenburg and Schleissheim, lived in England and spent the last seven years of his life in Madrid. His versatility – as a mural painter, as a portraitist and as a general purveyor of any type of picture his patron might demand – was as much a by-product of necessity as of choice. In England for instance, although he produced decorative schemes for Covent Garden and Moor Park, the more austere architectural tastes which were being fostered by Lord Burlington's circle forced him into portraiture.

The primacy which the Venetians had achieved by the eighteenth century in the field of decorative mural painting was obviously due in part to past traditions; to the great decorative schemes of the Doge's Palace, of the Scuola di San Rocco, and the great paintings of Veronese. But more specifically it owed a special debt to Sebastiano Ricci and his nephew Marco. Absorbing Veronese's decorative gifts, commanding a clear, bright range of colours, Sebastiano showed that intelligent awareness of the past which had been disseminated by the Carracci, and the influence of Bologna is very clear in his work. He spent two years in Vienna before coming to England in 1712 with Marco. The only surviving examples of his work in England are a ceiling in the Royal Academy and a painting of *The Resurrection* in the apse of the chapel of the Royal Hospital, Chelsea. On his return to Venice he painted a series of religious pictures, many of which were bought by Joseph Smith, the English consul there, and subsequently sold to George III. About forty landscapes painted by Marco, who tended to specialize in that genre, and showed in it a strong romantic tendency, similarly found their way into the English Royal Collection.

It is possible that without the Ricci the art of Giovanni Battista Tiepolo, who died in 1770 at the age of seventy-four, would have been less remarkable. In a sense Tiepolo was the last great practitioner of the Renaissance tradition, including in his work elements not only of Titian, Tintoretto and Veronese, but of Rubens and Rembrandt, of Dürer, and the masters of Roman Baroque. In his fantastic mastery of perspective he pushed to their most dizzying heights the visual techniques first explored by painters such as Uccello and Signorelli, but he reinforced them with those theatrical effects which were being perfected by the theatrical artists of his own age. He did, in fact, employ an expert in perspective, Geralamo Mangozzi-Colonna, a scientist and stage-manager, who advised him on some of his more elaborate schemes. He has no equal in the depiction of air-borne figures, which swirl through his paintings with a sense of delicious insouciance which adds so much to the charm of all his works. His nudes exude an aura of smiling sensuality, united with an engaging innocence which recalls the atmosphere of Giorgione's women. Although he was immensely successful throughout his long life, his last years in Madrid were clouded by the triumph of that

5

6

6. PIETRO LONGHI (1702–85)
The Concert
Oil on canvas, $23\frac{1}{2} \times 18\frac{3}{4}$ in (60 × 48 cm)
Gallerie dell' Accademia, Venice

Although the scene is one which must have been familiar in a Venice which adored music passionately, Longhi adds a touch of Hogarthian caricature, especially to the figures of the three clerics playing cards.

type of newly fashionable Neo-Classical painting practised by artists such as Mengs, which was in its scholarly severity so unlike his own exercises in luminous hedonism.

The dominant position which Venice held in the art of eighteenth-century Italy was, however, not due merely to the brilliance of its decorative painters. The growth of genre painting depicting scenes of ordinary life, often with a humorous undercurrent, had been continuous since the middle of the seventeenth century, marrying happily with those new strains of specifically Italian realism initiated by Caravaggio. Crespi, the Bolognese artist who had been influenced by Guercino, and whose works are often marked by a kind of Mannerist violence of colour accompanied by dramatic lighting and tumultuous compositional schemes, specialized in rather biting views of ordinary people. Among his many pupils was Pietro Longhi, whose paintings, delicately ironical, sharply observed, paralleled the works of Casanova and Goldoni in presenting us with a picture of Venice in the age of its glorious decay. Giovanni Battista Piazetta, who was one of the teachers of Tiepolo, had himself been a pupil of Crespi, but his output was far more varied, and his dramatic compositions on religious and historical themes, his illustrations and his famous charcoal drawings from the nude were better known in his own lifetime than were his paintings of contemporary life and the theatre.

Probably no city of the past is more widely known to us than eighteenth-century Venice; we are more familiar with its canals, its piazza, its campi than with the streets of any other city, thanks to the work of two of the most famous topographical artists Italy has ever produced – Canaletto and Guardi. Heirs of that tradition which had been established two centuries before by Carpaccio's paintings of the same city, they bore to each other the same kind of artistic relationship as that which existed between Claude and Poussin and between Constable and Turner. Trained in the topographical traditions of the Roman artists, Canaletto was immensely popular with the English; in the 1750s he spent many years in England and his works were bought so lavishly by the English that he is better represented in British than in Italian collections. His output was immense. The accuracy of his work, its regard for detail, its almost mechanical realism could lead at times to over-stylization and to an insensitive handling of paint, but at his best he was unrivalled and the influence which he exerted on the whole development of landscape painting is undeniable.

The Guardi brothers Francesco (1712–93) and Giannantonio, typified the kind of family nexus in the arts which had persisted since the Middle Ages. Their father, who came from the north, had set up a *bottega* in Venice in the 1690s and Giannantonio, the elder and less famous, probably trained Francesco, who started his career as a painter of religious and genre pictures, not turning to landscape and topography until he was in his late forties. Their sister, Cecilia, became Tiepolo's wife. As opposed to Canaletto, who was in his lifetime much more successful, Francesco Guardi was impressionistic in his technique, quick and emotional in his touch, always varied in his approach to places or people and able to depict scenes and actions with an absolute minimum of effort. His paintings which are vibrant with light and atmosphere have a much greater appeal to those generations which have come to appreciate the discoveries of the Impressionists, than they had when they were painted.

7

8

7. VITTORE GHISLANDI known as
FRA CALGARIO (1655–1743)
Portrait of Count Giovanni Battista Vailetti
Oil on canvas, $88\frac{3}{4} \times 53\frac{3}{4}$ in (226×137 cm)
Gallerie dell' Accademia, Venice

Painted about 1710, this portrait by a painter who lived and worked in Bergamo, must be considered one of the finest produced in eighteenth-century Italy. The attention paid to *the clothes which the Count is wearing is a remarkable feat of painterly virtuosity and the whole picture is alive with warmth and sumptuousness.*

8. SEBASTIANO RICCI (1660–1734)
The Dream of Aesculapius
Oil on canvas, $24\frac{1}{2} \times 39\frac{1}{4}$ in (62×100 cm)
Gallerie dell' Accademia, Venice

The loose impressionistic handling of the paint and the rapidity with which he establishes a sense of movement and *revelation, indicates the decorative nature of Ricci's talents and the effect it had on the younger generation.*

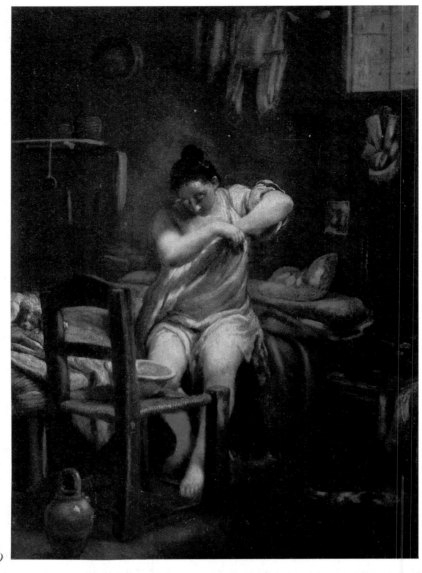

9

10

11

12

9. GIUSEPPE MARIA CRESPI
(1665–1747)
The Flea
Copper, $11 \times 9\frac{1}{4}$ in (28×24 cm)
Uffizi, Florence

A tiny painting which shows immense spatial depth, this work reflects the influence of Dutch and Flemish painting and is suggestive almost of an Italian Chardin. During the course of his life Crespi developed a vivid genre style.

10. ROSALBA CARRIERA (1678–1758)
Portrait of a Lady
Pastel on card, $21\frac{1}{2} \times 16\frac{1}{2}$ in (55×42 cm)
Gallerie dell' Accademia, Venice

Rosalba's delicate touch as a pastellist, her ability to portray and yet flatter, made her one of the most successful portraitists of the eighteenth century. Her greatest successes were in Vienna, Paris and with English visitors to Venice.

11. ROSALBA CARRIERA
Portrait of a Boy of the Leblond Family
Pastel on board, $13\frac{3}{4} \times 10\frac{1}{4}$ in (34×27 cm)
Gallerie dell' Accademia, Venice

The pale colouring of this French boy is enhanced by the light on his face and by the skill with which the artist has depicted the texture of his clothes in the difficult medium of pastel.

12. JACOPO AMIGONI (1675–1752)
Venus and Adonis
Oil on canvas, $17\frac{3}{4} \times 29\frac{1}{2}$ in (45×75 cm)
Gallerie dell' Accademia, Venice

Hinting at the influence he was to have on painters such as Boucher, this rather hackneyed treatment of a familiar mythological subject is redeemed by its fine atmospheric effects and radiant lighting.

13

14

13. MARCO RICCI (1679–1729)
Landscape with Figures
Detail of an oil on canvas, $53\frac{3}{4} \times 77\frac{1}{2}$ in
(137×197 cm)
Gallerie dell' Accademia, Venice

Influenced by the art of Alessandro Magnasco, which gave *feeling, Marco Ricci carried into the eighteenth century the*
his own landscape paintings a quick, nervously sensitive *traditional Venetian response to nature.*

14. GIOVANNI BATTISTA PIAZETTA
(1682–1754)
Susanna at the Bath
Oil on canvas, $39\frac{1}{4} \times 53$ in (100×135 cm)
Uffizi, Florence

An early work painted before 1720, this picture shows *and feeling for dramatic composition. The gestures of the*
Piazetta's mastery of plastic values, his fine sense of colour *Elders' hands are especially telling.*

15

15. GIAMBATTISTA PITTONI
(1687–1767)
The Annunciation
Oil on canvas, 60 × 81 in (153 × 206 cm)
Gallerie dell' Accademia, Venice

Seldom can an angel making an announcement to the Virgin Mary have been depicted in so sexually attractive a guise. *This delicious exercise in sensuous spirituality was painted for Pittoni's admission to the Venetian Academy in 1757.*

16. GIOVANNI BATTISTA TIEPOLO
(1696–1770)
Diana and Actaeon
Oil on canvas, 38¾ × 53 in (99 × 135 cm)
Gallerie dell' Accademia, Venice

Influenced by the luminosity of Sebastiano Ricci, and heir to the great traditions of Venetian decorative art, Tiepolo was not entirely at ease with single figures such as this. For his *art to reach its maximum potential he needed a crowded scene and ample space. There is, however, a very romantic feeling about the background to this work.*

17. GIOVANNI BATTISTA TIEPOLO
The Rape of Europa
Oil on canvas, 38¾ × 52½ in (99 × 134 cm)
Gallerie dell' Accademia, Venice

Tiepolo has treated this familiar theme with striking originality. Instead of the usual turbulent imagery of a bull *thundering off with the young lady, he shows her seated demurely at her toilet set in a charming landscape.*

16

17

18

18. PIETRO LONGHI (1702–85)
The Confession
Oil on canvas, 24 × 19½ in (61 × 50 cm)
Uffizi, Florence

Longhi made duplicates of many of his more successful paintings of Venetian social life and this seems to have been based on a prototype in the Accademia in Venice. His pictures were also very often copied by his pupils.

20

19. ANTONIO CANAL known as
CANALETTO (1697–1768)
View of a Palazzo
Oil on canvas, $51\frac{1}{2} \times 36\frac{1}{2}$ in (131 × 93 cm)
Gallerie dell' Accademia, Venice

This painting of an imaginary scene was the 'exercize in perspective' which the painter had to submit to gain admission to the Academy of Painting and Sculpture in *Venice, in 1765. Despite the fact that it does involve some elaborate perspective effects, it is much more free than many of his famous topographical paintings.*

20. MICHELE MARIESCHI (1710–43)
Fantastic Landscape with an Obelisk
Oil on canvas, $21\frac{1}{2} \times 32$ in (55 × 82 cm)
Gallerie dell' Accademia, Venice

Had he lived longer, Marieschi might well have outshone Canaletto as a topographical artist. This capriccio *shows his gifts at their most convincing. The decayed building on* *the right contains elements from the Doge's palace and the pulpit is based on that in San Marco. The landscape, however, seems to have been based on that near Lake Como.*

21. FRANCESCO GUARDI (1712–93)
Landscape with a Bridge and Canal
Oil on canvas, $11\frac{3}{4} \times 20\frac{3}{4}$ in (30 × 53 cm)
Uffizi, Florence

Probably a scene on the island of Murano, this delicate painting with its ravishing atmosphere, sensitive colouring *and quick impressionistic brushwork is typical of Guardi's genius at its best.*

21

22

22. FRANCESCO GUARDI
Arch and Seascape
Oil on canvas, $11\frac{3}{4} \times 20\frac{3}{4}$ in (30×53 cm)
Uffizi, Florence

One of those capricci *or imaginary landscapes so popular in eighteenth-century Venice, this example shows Guardi's* remarkable ability to paint sky and sea in an utterly convincing way.

23

23. ANTONIO CANOVA (1757–1822)
Pauline Borghese as Venus Victrix
Detail of a marble statue, 36 in (92 cm)
Galleria Borghese, Rome

The elegant statue of Bonaparte's sister Pauline, of which this is a detail, is the most celebrated work of the Italian Neo-Classical sculptor, Canova, who settled in Rome in *1781. Achieving an astonishing degree of artistic and social success, Canova dominated European sculpture for almost a century but is now criticized for sentimentality.*

24. ALESSANDRO LONGHI (1733–1813)
Portrait of Padre Carlo Lodoli
Oil on canvas, $51 \times 37\frac{1}{4}$ in (130×95 cm)
Gallerie dell' Accademia, Venice

A writer about architecture and a famous teacher, Fra Lodoli (1690–1771) was involved in many of the bitter artistic controversies which marked the eighteenth century. Alles- *sandro Longhi, the son of Pietro, was official portrait painter to the Venetian Academy and himself a writer on artistic personalities in contemporary Venice.*

24

VII

A European Legacy Preserved

In 1796, three years after the death of Francesco Guardi, Napoleon invaded Italy. This was an event which was to alter the history of the nation and was to have an influence on its artistic heritage which was initially disastrous, but in the long run beneficial. Preoccupied with making Paris the artistic as well as the political capital of Europe, Napoleon looted the art treasures of every country which fell to the French with a voracity which makes later predators, such as Goering, seem like petty pilferers. Pope Pius VII was required to hand over:

> 'one hundred pictures, busts, vases or statues to be chosen by the Commissioners of the French Nation, among which would be the bronze bust of Junius Brutus and the marble bust of Marcus Brutus from the Capitol, and five hundred manuscripts to be chosen by the said Commissioners.'[1]

The famous bronze horses were removed from the porch of San Marco in Venice, and the major works of Titian, Tintoretto and Veronese were appropriated. The same pattern of spoliation was inflicted on Ravenna, Florence, Perugia and Milan, and this vast body of loot was sent by sea to Marseilles and then floated up the Rhone and other waterways to Paris, where it arrived on 27 July, 1798. Mounted on triumphant chariots decorated with leaves and banners proclaiming the contents of each case, they were carried in procession to the Louvre, which was being converted into that great public museum which we know today. The museum was initially under the direction of Ennio Quirino Visconti, whose father Giovanni Battista had been one of the first official curators of the Vatican Museums, and then of Baron Vivant-Denon, the virtual creator of the concept of the public museum and art gallery. On the eventual downfall of Napoleon the allies agreed with Lord Liverpool that:

> 'it is most desirable to remove these trophies (i.e. the looted works of art) from France, as whilst in that country they must necessarily have the effect of keeping up the memory of their former conquests, and of cherishing the military spirit and vanity of the nation.'[2]

At one point it was suggested that the *Belvedere Apollo* be given to the Prince Regent, but it was eventually decided that:

1. ALBRECHT DÜRER (1471–1528)
The Apostle Philip
Oil on canvas, 18 × 14¾ in (46 × 38 cm)
Uffizi, Florence

This painting is an example of Dürer's style when he was tending to stress linear form and two-dimensional decorative qualities at the expense of colour and plasticity. It was executed in 1516 when Dürer was working for the Emperor Maximilian as Court Painter. He later became Court Painter to his successor, Charles V.

2

2. ANTONIO CANOVA (1757–1822)
Pauline Borghese as Venus Victrix
Marble, 36 in (92 cm)
Galleria Borghese, Rome

Canova's famous statue has conferred on Napoleon's lascivious sister an immortality which she may have expected but did not merit. One of the great monuments of Neo-classicism, *this work combines Hellenistic elegance with human warmth and is the best known commission Canova received from Napoleon's family.*

'His Royal Highness' sentiments are far too dignified to accept a present which would be too generally deemed to be a bribe.'[3]

Restitution took place on a massive scale, but even so, the Louvre retained about thirty important paintings, including works by Botticelli, Giotto, Cimabue and Piero di Cosimo – artists whose real worth at that time was only appreciated by a small number of connoisseurs. The sculptor, Antonio Canova, was sent to Paris with the rank of ambassador to negotiate the details of the return of Italy's art treasures, and for his success was made Marchese d'Ischia by the Pope in 1816. Rivalling Bernini in the degree of popular success and recognition which he received, Canova worked for patrons from most European countries and the United States. He had been lavishly patronized by the Bonaparte family, especially by the Emperor's sister Pauline, who had married Prince Camillo Borghese and has left in the Villa that memorably erotic statue of herself as a recumbent Venus by Canova. Although as assiduous in his study of the classic past as any Renaissance master, Canova may well be thought of as the first modern sculptor, emphasizing form rather than content, insisting on a multiple viewpoint and outdoing the masters of the Baroque in the virtuosity with which he achieved the most dazzling balancing effects.

Canova had spent his early working life in Venice and during the Paris negotiations had been especially concerned with the horses of San Marco. These had been dismembered on Napoleon's instructions and handed over to the Austrians, indicating the special hatred he seemed to bear towards the Republic. It is significant that it was in Venice therefore that one of the first positive consequences of the Napoleonic episode was experienced. The mere existence of the Louvre had established a prototype for a museum dedicated rather to the pleasure of the populace than the private delights of the rich and powerful. In Italy there was also the added incentive that with the growth of an aggressive, self-conscious national spirit a new awareness of the greatness of the country's artistic legacy provided a spiritual rallying point. This was especially so in Venice, where churches and *Scuole* had been ravished by the French, abetted in some instances by less scrupulous citizens of the Republic who were not averse to adorning their homes with any accessible spoils. Peter Edwards, a Venetianized Englishman and Leopoldo Cicognara, the President of the Venetian Academy of Art which had been established in 1750 under the presidency of Piazzetta, were entrusted with salvaging what they could of the paintings of the past. By 1817, with the active help and guidance of Canova, they had secured a cluster of buildings facing the Palazzo Barbaro: the Church of Charity, the Monastery of the Canons of the Lateran and the Scuola Granda di Santa Maria della Carita, which were joined together by the architect G.A. Selva to form what was basically the gallery of the Accademia as we know it today. The original stock of works was increased during the first few decades of the gallery's existence by important donations from old ducal families such as the Contarini, and so Venice at last had a gallery of its own, the last of the great Italian art centres to do so.

If Venice was the most nationally minded of the Italian cities, Rome was probably the least, but its fame as a centre of art had grown throughout the eighteenth century, partly in response to the increasing number of travellers who came there, partly through the great strides which were made in art scholarship and a widening appreciation of painting, which would lead eventually to the rediscovery of the beauties of these 'primitives' who came before Michelangelo and Raphael. The care and arrangement of the papal collections including some two hundred Greek and Etruscan vases.

Another complex of galleries was built in the reign of Pius VI (1775–99) who filled it with about six hundred newly acquired works, and opened it to the general public in 1787 under the title of the Museo Pio-Clementino. When the works looted by the French were returned they were housed in a Braccio Nouvo (New Wing) which took the larger and more important pieces of sculpture, and an Art Gallery (Pinacoteca) which was housed in varying parts of the Vatican until it was given a permanent home by Pius XI in 1932. The Napoleonic depredations had in the long run increased the papal collections; Pius VII (1800–23) actively encouraged fresh excavations and bought extensively on the art market to make good some of the losses, and when the stolen paintings were returned, many, such as Raphael's *Transfiguration* and Caravaggio's *Deposition* were not placed in their original sites in various cities of the Papal States, but were kept in the Vatican.

Other additions made to the Vatican museums during the pontificate of Gregory XVI (1831–46) were the Etruscan Museum which was enriched as a consequence of the legislation of one of his predecessors forbidding the export of excavated works of art, which until that time had been going to countries such as England in prolific abundance, and an Egyptian Museum, the most important of its kind in Italy. Of course the main sites of excavation, especially since the discovery of the buried towns around

Vesuvius, had been in the south of the country. In this matter at least the Bourbons had a fairly good record. Tyrannical rulers of the Kingdom of the Two Sicilies they may have been, but they fostered archaeological zeal and took steps to display its fruits in what had originally been the Università di Studi into the Museo Borbonico between 1780 and 1820. Eventually this became the Museo Nazionale, but today it still retains very much the same appearance as it had in the late eighteenth century.

The growth of railways, the introduction of cheap excursions on the pattern created by Thomas Cook, the first English tourist agent, and the spread of popular education had as important an effect on the tourist invasion of Italy as the introduction of cheap air fares was to have a century later. Baedeker's guide books, the writings of critics such as Ruskin, of art historians such as Crowe and Cavalcaselle whose enormously influential books on the history of Italian paintings were published between 1865 and 1870, and of writers such as Dickens and Mark Twain who wrote travel books about Italy, contributed still further to the popularity of museums and art galleries, which were increasingly coming to be controlled either by the State or by local municipalities. In Florence the Uffizi had always been accessible to visitors, as the writings of Evelyn and Addison, as well as Zoffany's famous painting of the interior of the gallery record. In 1798 the Pitti, which until then had been treated as the private collection of the Grand Dukes, was thrown open to the public and arranged as a museum. Its collections were enriched still further in the nineteenth century by the Grand Duke Ferdinand II, who acquired works by Van Dyck, Salvator Rosa and the Rembrandt *Self-portrait*. Further treasures were added to both galleries (as well as to other Italian museums) as a result of the temporary suppression of religious orders in 1886.

For generations of English and Americans Italy has become to some an actual, to others an ideal homeland. Its art treasures are seen every year by millions of visitors disgorged by plane, boat and train. Preserved with the aid of all the resources known to a technologically minded society, housed in buildings which are as beautiful and artistically significant as their contents, four thousand years of Italian art have become part of the legacy of the whole world.

3. SIR ANTHONY VAN DYCK
(1599–1641)
Cardinal Guido Bentivoglio
Oil on canvas, $76\frac{1}{2} \times 57\frac{3}{4}$ in (195 × 147 cm)
Pitti, Florence

Guido Bentivoglio had been Papal Nuncio in Flanders and then in France before being made Cardinal in 1621. A powerful political personality, he made an ideal subject for one of Van Dyck's most masterly portraits.

3

4

5

4. HANS HOLBEIN (1497–1543)
Portrait of Sir Richard Southwell
Panel, $18\frac{1}{2} \times 14\frac{3}{4}$ in (47×38 cm)
Uffizi, Florence

This fine portrait of a noted Tudor politician who was a member of Henry VIII's Privy Council, has an interesting history. It was given by Thomas Howard, Earl of Arundel, to the Grand Duke Cosimo in 1621, after he had expressed a desire to own a portrait by the artist. Arundel was one of the first great English collectors and connoisseurs and spent much of his life in Italy where his activities included buying pictures and other objects of virtu for Charles I.

5. JOOS VAN CLEVE (c.1485–1540)
Portrait of a Woman
Panel, $22\frac{1}{2} \times 16\frac{1}{2}$ in (57×42 cm)
Uffizi, Florence

Painted in 1520, this serene Flemish work reflects the fact that the artist probably saw Leonardo's work on a visit to Italy and was influenced by it. Cleve became a Master in Antwerp in 1511 and is thought to have worked at the court of François I of France c1530. Unfortunately none of Joos' portraits can be directly authenticated.

6. SIR PETER PAUL RUBENS
(1577–1640)
The Four Philosophers
Panel, $64\frac{1}{2} \times 54\frac{1}{2}$ in (164×139 cm)
Pitti, Florence

Although this is the usually accepted title, the painting actually depicts the artist himself (on the left) his younger brother Philip, the philosopher Justus Lipsius and Jan van de Wouvere, whom the painter had met at Verona in 1602.

6

7

8

9

7. PAUL BRILL (1554–1626)
Landscape with Deer Hunters
Detail of an oil on canvas, 8 × 11 in (21 × 28 cm)
Pitti, Florence

There are still elements of the Flemish tradition apparent in this detail, but there is also evident something of that serenity which was to make Brill an important influence on painters such as Claude. A prolific painter of landscape pictures for the tourist trade in Rome, whence he had moved from Antwerp c1575, Brill was influenced by Elsheimer and Annibale Carracci and successfully bridged the gap between Mannerist and seventeenth-century landscape.

8. SIR PETER PAUL RUBENS
(1577–1640)
Peasants Returning from the Fields
Panel, 47½ × 76¼ in (121 × 194 cm)
Pitti, Florence

Probably painted in 1637 and showing the town of Malines in the left background, this fine landscape reflects Rubens' ability to achieve impressive effects of light and atmosphere even late in his career.

9. SIR PETER PAUL RUBENS
Isabella Brandt
Panel, 33¾ × 24½ in (86 × 62 cm)
Uffizi, Florence

A simple and moving portrait of the artist's first wife, who died in 1626. After marrying Isabella Brandt in 1609, Rubens built himself a magnificent Italianate house in Antwerp and embarked on one of the most vigorous careers.

10

11

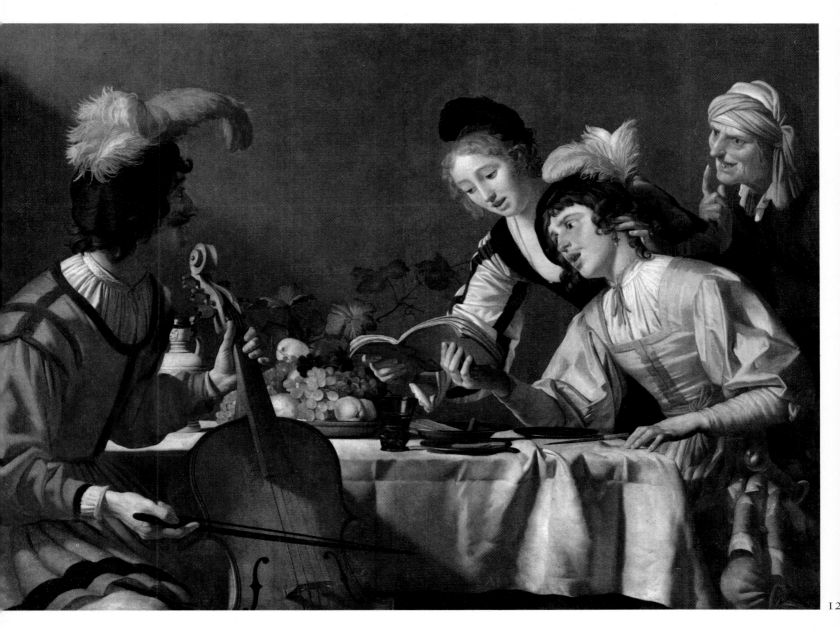

12

10. JAN LYS or LISS (c.1580–1629)
Abel Mourned by His Parents
Oil on canvas, 26¼ × 33 in (67 × 84 cm)
Gallerie dell' Accademia, Venice

Although born at Holstein and studying under Goltzius at Amsterdam, Lys spent most of his working life in Italy, first in Rome, where he fell under the spell of Caravaggio, and then in Venice, where he died.

11. JUSEPE RIBERA called SPAGNOLETTO (1588–1652)
The Martyrdom of St. Bartholomew
Oil on canvas, 57 × 85 in (145 × 216 cm)
Pitti, Florence

Born in Valencia, Ribera later moved to Italy and settled in Naples which was then a Spanish province. He became immensely popular in the wake of Caravaggio and his dramatic paintings, with their emphatic lighting, are marked by the quick spontaneity of the brushwork and dramatic flair.

12. GERARD HONTHORST
(1590–1656)
A Concert
Oil on canvas, 66 × 78 in (168 × 202 cm)
Galleria Borghese, Rome

This picture was bought by Cardinal Scipione Borghese when the artist was working in Rome between c1610 and 1620. In works such as this Honthorst gave a Flemish impetus to the taste for genre paintings which was developing in Italy about this time. Although he never met Caravaggio, who had died before his arrival in Italy, Honthorst was obviously deeply influenced by him as this painting shows. The psychological realism of which Caravaggio was a master can be seen, for example, in the way in which the girl's fingers caress the young man.

313

13

14

13. REMBRANDT VAN RYN (1606–69)
Self-portrait as an Old Man
Oil on canvas, $43\frac{1}{2} \times 38$ in (111×97 cm)
Uffizi, Florence

Glowing with internal light and painted at the comparatively early age of 58, this is one of that magnificent series of exercises in self scrutiny which Rembrandt carried out late in his career.

14. SIR ANTHONY VAN DYCK
(1599–1641)
Portrait of Giovanni di Montfort
Oil on canvas, 48×35 in (122×89 cm)
Uffizi, Florence

Van Dyck captures perfectly the sense of self-sufficiency, power and authority which emanate from the sitter. Yet all is done with a perfect economy of means and with a highly characteristic elegance.

15. JUSTUS SUSTERMANS (1597–1681)
Prince Mattias de' Medici
Oil on canvas, 30 × 23½ in (76 × 60 cm)
Pitti, Florence

Sustermans, who was born in Antwerp, arrived in Florence in 1620 and for the next sixty years worked there, mainly as *Court Painter to the Medici. Prince Mattias was a younger son of Duke Cosimo II.*

16. JUSTUS SUSTERMANS
Ferdinando II de' Medici
Oil on canvas, 30½ × 26 in (78 × 66 cm)
Pitti, Florence

The Medici face which looks at us with thoughtful disdain from above the finely damascened armour, is that of another son of Cosimo II. Ferdinando married Vittoria della *Rovere, who brought as her dowry the famous art collection of the Dukes of Urbino, which became part of the Medici treasures.*

18

17. JEAN BAPTISTE CHARDIN
(*c*.1699–1779)
The Game of Shuttlecock
Oil on canvas, $31\frac{3}{4} \times 25\frac{1}{2}$ in (81 × 65 cm)
Uffizi, Florence

Chardin carried on into the eighteenth century that tradition of genre painting which had evolved in the Low Countries in the previous century, but endowed it with greater simplicity and human charm.

18. JAN STEEN (*c*.1626–1679)
The Meal
Panel, $19\frac{1}{2} \times 16$ in (50 × 41 cm)
Uffizi, Florence

The most versatile of Dutch artists and one of the most prolific, Steen specialized in this type of theatrically lit genre scene which must have appealed to a generation seduced by the realism of Caravaggio.

ACKNOWLEDGMENTS

The photographs in this book were supplied by Archivio I.G.D.A., Milan.

The author would like to acknowledge the help and co-operation of
his wife Joan, and the tireless and unselfish work of Margaret Brenton,
without which this work might never have been completed.

NOTES

INTRODUCTION
1 Tatham, E.R.H. *Francesco Petrarca* London 1925, Vol. 1,
p.338.

THE CLASSICAL HERITAGE
1 The history of this piece shows how richly complex the career
of a work of art can be. Caesar obtained it from Mark Antony,
who had found it in Samos. On Caesar's death Augustus placed
it in the Capitol in Rome, where it stayed until the sixteenth
century when it was appropriated by Margaret of Antich,
Duchess of Camarion. She gave it to Cardinal Granvelle
(1517–86) the governor of the Netherlands under Charles V,
who placed it in the gardens of his castle at Besançon. When
Louis XIV took the city in the seventeenth century, the citizens
presented it to him, and it was placed in the gardens at Versailles,
and from there it found its way into the Louvre.
2 Lewis, J.D. (translator), *Letters of Pliny the Younger* London
1879, p.214.
3 Seneca quoted in Hauser, Arnold *A Social History of Art*
London 1962, Vol 1, p.107.

HEAVEN ON EARTH
1 Boccaccio, Giovanni *Decameron* Everyman edition, Dent,
London 1953, Vol 2, pp.73–4.
2 Petrarch quoted in Larner, John *Culture and Society in Italy
1290–1420* London 1971, p.277.
3 Origo, Iris *The Merchant of Prato* London 1963.
4 *op.cit.*

THE TRIUMPH OF THE EYE
1 Machiavelli quoted in Taylor, Francis Henry *The Taste of
Angels* Hamish Hamilton, London 1948, p.92.
2 Clark, Kenneth *The Nude* Princeton, 1972, pp.26–27.
3 Vasari, Giorgio *The Lives of the Most Eminent Painters, Sculptors
and Architects*, Everyman edition, London 1963, Vol 2, p.82.
4 da Vinci, Leonardo *Notebooks* Edited by MacCurdy, E.,
London 1977, Vol 2, p.265.
5 Vasari, Giorgio *The Lives of the Most Eminent Painters, Sculptors
and Architects* Everyman edition, London 1963.
6 Naldi, Naldo quoted in Gombrich, E.H. *Symbolic Images*
Phaidon Press, London & New York 1972, p.206.

7 *op. cit.* p. 47.
8 *The Works of Apuleius*, Loeb Classical Library, London &
New York 1919, p.524.
9 de' Medici, Cosimo quoted in Wackernagel, Martin *Des
Lebensraum des Kunstlers in der Florentinischen Renaissance* Leipsig
1938, p.234.
10 d'Este, Isabella quoted in Cartwright, Julia *Isabella d'Este*
London & New York 1903, pp.137–8.
11 *op.cit.*
12 *op.cit.* p.179.
13 Singleton, C.S. (ed.) Castiglione, Baldessare *The Book of the
Courtier* Doubleday, New York 1959, p.121.

POPES AND PAINTERS
1 Michelangelo quoted in Osborne, Harold (ed.) *The Oxford
Companion to Art* Oxford 1970, p.720.
2 Cecchi, Emilio *Jacopo da Pontormo; Diario* Florence 1956;
quoted in Wittkower, E. *Born Under Saturn* Routledge & Kegan
Paul, London 1963, pp.70–1.
3 Mercer, Eric *Oxford History of English Art 1553–1625*, Oxford
1962, p.264.

PASSION AND ECSTASY
1 Schroeder, H.J. (translator) *Canons and Decrees of the Council of
Trent* St. Louis & London 1941, p.87.
2 Holt, E.G. *Literary Sources of Art History* Princeton University
Press, 1947, p.56.
3 de Pittori, Vite *Sculptori et architetti Moderni* Rome 1672.

THE KINGDOM OF THE SENSES
1 Bray, William (ed.) *The Diary of John Evelyn* London, n.d.,
pp.98–9.

A LEGACY PRESERVED
1 Mackay Quynn, Dorothy 'The Art Confiscations of the
Napoleonic Wars' in *The American Historical Review* April 1945.
2 Taylor, Francis Henry *The Taste of Angels* Hamish Hamilton,
London 1948.
3 *op.cit.* p.572.

page 318 PAOLO VERONESE (*c.*1528–88)

The Annunciation

Oil on canvas, 56¼ × 114¼ in (143 × 291 cm)

Uffizi, Florence

A youthful work of the artist, this spacious, beautifully lit composition shows his remarkable ability to create a dramatically convincing image of a familiar theme. The *vases of flowers on the left and the finely contrived perspective view in the centre of the picture are particularly worthy of note.*

page 319 JACOBELLO ALBEREGNO (*fl.*1397)

Christ on the Cross with the Virgin and John the
Baptist

Panel, 17 × 24in (45 × 56cm)

Gallerie dell' Accademia, Venice

The painter of this poignantly dignified picture is a comparatively little known Venetian master with an interesting output of religious works often containing some *macabre element. Here Christ's blood flows freely on to a skull buried beneath the Cross, perhaps as a symbol of Christ's blood saving mankind from everlasting death.*

page 320 GIOVANNI BELLINI (*c.*1430–1516)

A Sacred Allegory

Panel 44¾ × 83¾ in (114 × 213 cm)

Uffizi, Florence

Painted c.1488, this mysteriously evocative painting displays the sense of colour and the feeling for the natural beauty of landscape which had already become the hallmarks of Venetian art. The enigmatic nature of the subject is enhanced by the luminous clarity of the whole *composition. Giovanni Bellini pioneered a new convention of allegorical painting which was far less tied to precise literary texts than ever before. He was thus free to invent a world of his own, in which we should probably not look for specific coded meanings.*

INDEX TO ARTISTS